Data Protection
for voluntary organisations

Paul Ticher

DIRECTORY OF SOCIAL CHANGE

in association with
Bates, Wells & Braithwaite

Published by
The Directory of Social Change
24 Stephenson Way
London NW1 2DP
tel: 020 7209 5151, fax: 020 7209 5049
e-mail: info@dsc.org.uk
from whom further copies and a full publications list are available.

The Directory of Social Change is a Registered Charity no. 800517

ISBN 1 900360 47 0

British Library Cataloguing in Publication Data
A catalogue record for this book is available from the British Library

Designed by Sarah Nicholson
Typeset by Tradespools Ltd., Frome
Printed and bound by Antony Rowe, Chippenham

Other Directory of Social Change departments in London:
Courses and Conferences tel: 020 7209 4949
Charity Centre tel: 020 7209 1015
Research tel: 020 7209 4422
Finance and Administration tel: 020 7209 0902

Directory of Social Change Northern Office:
Federation House, Hope Street, Liverpool L1 9BW
Courses and Conferences tel: 0151 708 0117
Research tel: 0151 708 0136

Contents

Acknowledgements

The author would like to thank all those who have contributed to the book, especially those participants on training courses and briefing sessions whose acute questions and real-life examples have done so much to stimulate his thinking about Data Protection.

Special mention must also go to Stephen Lloyd of Bates Wells & Braithwaite for reading the book in draft and providing a welcome legal perspective. Any remaining errors and misunderstandings are, of course, the responsibility of the author alone.

Please note that this book does not set out to be a full statement of the law, and is not a substitute for professional legal advice on specific issues.

About the author

Paul Ticher is a consultant and trainer working with national and local voluntary organisations. He specialises in information technology and good practice in information management, with a particular interest in data protection. Much of his work experience has been in the advice and information field, including five years as IT adviser at the Community Information project (now absorbed into London Advice Services Alliance), where he undertook a considerable amount of work on the application of the 1984 Data Protection Act to voluntary organisations when it was first introduced. He has also worked in campaigning organisations and as Chief Officer of a small national charity.

e-mail: paul@ptgt.dircon.co.uk

Definitions and abbreviations

Terms used in this book are defined below, or explained at the pages indicated.

The Act – the 1998 Data Protection Act.

Computer – used as a shorthand term in several places in this book. The Act refers to 'equipment operating automatically in response to instructions given for that purpose'.

Data – *see page 1.*

Data capture – the process of obtaining information from the **Data Subject**, either on paper forms or verbally, often used in the context of the **Data Controller**'s first contact with that person.

Data Controller – *see page 7.*

Data Processor – *see page 9.*

Data Protection Commissioner – the official responsible for enforcing Data Protection law, known as the Data Protection Registrar before 1 March 2000.

Data Protection Registrar – *see **Data Protection Commissioner** above.*

Data User – the 1984 Act equivalent of a **Data Controller**, *see page 7.*

Data Subject – *see page 4.*

Direct Marketing – 'the communication (by whatever means) of any advertising or marketing material which is directed to particular individuals', *see page 37.*

EU Directive 95/46/EC – the Directive, approved by the European Union on 24 October 1995, under which all member states had to bring in similar Data Protection legislation within three years. Limited areas were left to national discretion, but the main provisions apply throughout the European Union.

EU Directive 97/66/EC – the Directive under which tele-marketing is regulated, *see page 38.*

Manual records – used in this book (unless the context requires otherwise) to mean personal data held in a 'relevant filing system', *see page 2.*

Notification – the name under the 1998 Act for the equivalent to Registration under the 1984 Act. Some, but not all, Data Controllers have to 'notify' the Data Protection Commissioner about the broad outline of their data processing activities.

Processing – *see page 18.*

Record – used in this book to mean a set of information about one individual.

Relevant filing system – *see page 2.*

Sensitive personal data – *see page 24.*

Introduction
Data Protection

Data Protection is a somewhat contradictory subject – it can come over as terribly dry and procedural, but it goes to the heart of very real individual concerns, with potentially serious impact on people's lives. If your GP transfers your records to computer and the old paper files end up in a skip for anyone to see, that's a Data Protection issue. If your bank confuses you with someone else and your credit rating plummets, that's also a Data Protection issue.

For voluntary organisations, building a relationship of trust with clients, volunteers and donors is not just desirable, but essential. Good Data Protection practice is an important part of this equation.

The UK has had Data Protection legislation since 1984, but the 1998 Data Protection Act sees a new departure: a Data Protection regime which offers genuine new rights to Data Subjects as well as providing a framework for responsible behaviour by those using personal data. The new regime was not implemented until nearly ten years after its initiation within the European Union. However, there has been considerable consultation at various stages along the way, and the resulting legislation, while it could never be 'perfect', is workable and reasonable.

Voluntary organisations have no reason to fear the 1998 Act. In many ways it brings the law into line with good practices which have been developed and promoted in the sector ever since the 1984 Act. Compliance with the bureaucratic requirements is now, if anything, easier. This leaves Data Protection Officers free to concentrate on ensuring that their organisations have policies and procedures which genuinely protect the interests of Data Subjects.

At the heart of the Act is the concept of 'fairness'. If you handle information about people you have an overriding obligation to be fair. This means: ensuring that people know what is going on; using their data in predictable ways; looking after the data and taking care that it doesn't get into the wrong hands. And who could argue with that? It's no more than what we would expect from anyone who holds data about us.

Organisations which use data about individuals are faced with three options.

- Most voluntary organisations will be keen to follow best practice. This is not necessarily any more expensive than making the effort to find technical loopholes. It is the approach favoured in this book.
- Grudging compliance is an option for those wishing to circumvent the spirit of the new Act. As with any law, there are grey areas and special cases which can be exploited to avoid giving people the maximum benefit from the law.

- Ignoring the legislation has apparently been possible up to now for many of those who should have complied with the 1984 Act, but is obviously not recommended.

While good practice will not be very far from what many voluntary organisations are doing already, there are compliance issues to be aware of. There are even a very few circumstances in which Data Protection considerations may conflict with other concerns. (These are discussed at the appropriate points in the book.)

This book does not strictly follow the structure of the Act. Instead, it takes the reader step by step through the decision-making process in what is hoped is the most logical way. References to the text of the Act are made when appropriate, but the Act is not quoted in full.

It is important to be aware that the Data Protection Act has not been in force for long, and much of it has therefore not been tested in the Courts. This means that its interpretation is often more of an art than a science. Much of our current understanding of the Act is based on guidance from the Data Protection Commissioner. While authoritative, this is not legally binding. It is quite possible that the guidance might change, or be overturned by legal decisions. Day-to-day experience with the new Act will also contribute significantly to ideas on how best to put it into practice.

Readers are invited to contact the author with comments, or to seek further help on issues which are not adequately covered here. These points – and the other developments which will inevitably take place – can be taken into account if and when a second edition is prepared.

Structure of the book

The 1998 Data Protection Act (generally referred to as 'the Act' in this book) sets out to provide a framework for the use of data about people. It aims to be fair to the individuals concerned without unduly hampering the person or organisation using the data, provided that their activities are reasonable.

All words and phrases in **bold** in this section are defined and discussed in more detail in later chapters. (See also page vii for an index of definitions and abbreviations.)

The Act applies to **personal data;** that is, information about identifiable, living individuals which is held on computer or in many manual filing systems. The organisations or individuals which decide why and how personal data is **processed** (used in any way) are **Data Controllers.**

Chapter 1 looks in more detail at the definition of personal data, while Chapter 2 is concerned with identifying the Data Controller, in both straightforward and more complicated cases.

All Data Controllers have to follow the eight **Data Protection Principles**, a set of basic rules. These cover issues such as how to ensure fairness, the responsibility of the Data Controller to have good-quality data, and the Data Controller's security obligations. Chapter 3 looks briefly at all of the Principles.

Chapters 4 and 5 examine the issues surrounding 'fair' processing, particularly in relation to **sensitive data** – information about the Data Subject's racial or ethnic origin, beliefs, politics, health, sex life and criminal record. There are restrictions on using sensitive data, especially without the consent of the Data Subject.

In many situations getting the **consent** of the Data Subject is either necessary or advisable, but 'consent' is quite a tricky subject. When you might need it, and how you might get it, is discussed in Chapter 6.

Among the new rights that the Act gives to Data Subjects is an absolute right to stop the Data Controller using their data for **direct marketing** – including charity fundraising and other common activities of voluntary organisations. This is examined in Chapter 7.

One of the principle requirements for fairness is that the Data Controller must ensure that the **Data Subject** knows who is processing data about them and what for. There are particular requirements to provide information when sensitive data is being processed, when data might be used for direct marketing, and when it might be passed on to other organisations or people. Chapter 8 summarises these considerations and looks at the kind of information the Data Controller ought to be providing to the Data Subject in various circumstances, and how it might be provided.

Chapter 9 summarises the main Data Subject rights under the Act, while Chapter 10 examines one of the most important: the right of **Subject Access**, allowing people to see the data that is held about them.

Still with the Data Protection Principles, Chapter 11 considers the question of security, while Chapter 12 discusses the restrictions in the Act on transfer of data abroad.

Many Data Controllers will have to **notify** the **Data Protection Commissioner** about their data-processing activities. This is covered in Chapter 13, while Chapter 14 looks at the enforcement powers of the Data Protection Commissioner.

Although the 1998 Act applies to far more data and more activities than the 1984 Act, there are limited exemptions from parts of the Act, discussed in Chapter 15. Chapter 16 rounds off the main part of the book by offering a checklist of the responsibilities that are likely to apply in specific areas of work.

Most processing of personal data either has to comply with the Act immediately, or it will make sense to treat it as such. There are transition arrangements, however, which certain activities can benefit from until 24 October 2001. Chapter 17 looks briefly at these.

Background

The United Kingdom got its first Data Protection law – fittingly, as it seemed at the time – in 1984, the year of George Orwell's Big Brother. The law was introduced in order to allow the government to ratify a Data Protection Convention that had been drawn up by the Council of Europe. The limitations of the 1984 Act quickly became apparent. For organisations using data about people it imposed bureaucratic burdens, while offering very little benefit to individuals concerned about how their data was being used.

Very early in the life of the 1984 Act, criticisms began to emerge. At its heart it did very little to promote good practice in the use and management of personal data. Although it was based on fairly sound Data Protection principles, it allowed a Data User[1] to do more or less anything they wanted, provided that it was legal and that they had registered with the Data Protection Registrar in very broad terms what they intended to do.

The information a Data User had to provide was so general and unspecific that it gave very little information to anyone seriously interested in finding out anything about a data-processing operation. At the same time, filling in the forms was confusing and frustrating, and – particularly for small voluntary organisations – the registration fee was a significant disincentive. Hardly surprisingly, only an estimated 40% of those legally required to register actually did so.

A Data Subject wanting to check up on the data held about them could be faced with paying one organisation several, or in some cases even dozens, of £10 fees in order to cover all the possibilities. It is said that to see all the information held on one person by the Metropolitan Police could have cost £350.

On top of all this, the enforcement powers of the Data Protection Registrar were limited. Despite the heroic efforts at persuasion by successive Registrars, and their judicious use of the legal powers available, Data Protection under the 1984 Act never had much real day-to-day impact.

---

[1] Under the 1984 Act a Data User is any organisation or person who 'holds or controls' personal data. The 1998 Act equivalent is a Data Controller.

The limitations of the 1984 Act were widely acknowledged within a short time, and pressure grew for the most obvious problems, at least, to be ameliorated. However, the Home Office took the view that it did not want to legislate again in this area too quickly. Quite soon, the European Union began debating harmonisation of its Data Protection laws, and this was then given as a valid reason for making no change in the UK, only to have to make another set of changes once the European position was finalised.

Unfortunately, while the debate in Europe dragged on well into the 1990s, the Home Office steadfastly stood by its decision to wait. Because even the very fine detail of the 1984 Act was enshrined in the primary legislation itself, even the most obvious changes could not be made without recourse to Parliament. The Data Protection Registrars did the best they could – for example to simplify the registration process – but had very limited room for manoeuvre.

Eventually on 24 October 1995 the European Union agreed Directive 95/46/EC on the harmonisation of Data Protection laws. This gave member states three years to enact domestic legislation to put the Directive into effect. The UK government was still unenthusiastic about Europe, and dragged its feet – even for a while considering minor amendments to the 1984 Act rather than the wholesale revision that was merited.

For some, this turned out to be a blessing in disguise, as it gave a clean start to the new government which took office in May 1997. Commendably quickly, in August 1997, there appeared a White Paper, committing the government to implementing the spirit as well as the letter of the European Directive. This was followed, after a short period of consultation, by a Bill which had its first reading in January 1998.

Instead of incorporating all the detail into the Bill, as had been done in 1984, the 1998 legislation laid down a broad structure, leaving much of the detail to be completed through secondary legislation. This has the important advantage that if changes have to be made in future, they can be brought in much more easily, without the need for a new law. We should no longer have to live with unworkable provisions, merely because the effort of changing them is judged to be not worth it.

However, an unfortunate consequence was that Royal Assent for the new law on 16 July 1998 was not the end of the story. The law could not take effect until some thirty pieces of secondary legislation had been prepared, consulted on, and brought before Parliament. Despite the deadline set in the European Directive, the UK – in common with most other EU member states – started to fall behind schedule. In fact it was 1 March 2000 before the Act finally came into effect.

Has all the effort been worth it? There is no doubt that the new legislation does overcome many of the most obvious flaws in the old Act.

- Data Subjects are given real, if limited, controls over how their information is used.
- There is provision for much greater transparency: Data Subjects should know much more from now on about who is doing what with information about them.
- The impenetrable and unhelpful format for Registration has been replaced with a slightly simpler system of notification.
- Above all, the Act now incorporates much good practice. In the past, complying with the Act and following good practice, while by no means mutually exclusive, were almost two separate exercises.

The new Act requires all those who use personal data – not just those who hold it on computer and not just those who have to notify – to be fair and responsible in the way they use it.

Whatever flaws and problems emerge over the coming years, the 1998 Act is a much better starting point for all concerned – both those who use data about people, and the people whose data is being used.

What is personal data?

The 1998 Data Protection Act is concerned with 'personal data'. The 'personal' part is relatively straightforward, referring to data about:

- identifiable ■ living ■ individuals.

It therefore does not apply to information about companies or organisations, but it could apply to named contacts within those organisations. It does not apply to data which is completely anonymous, but it does apply if you can identify the people from the data combined with other information you hold. It does not apply to historical information about people who have died, or to fictitious people.

'Data' is a much trickier concept. It is defined in the Act under four headings. The full definition is given in the box, but for most purposes data essentially amounts to:

- information held on computer;
- information in 'relevant' manual files;
- information intended to become part of one of the above systems;
- certain information held by government and local government agencies to which the Data Subject has a right of access under other legislation.

Data[2]

means information which:

(a) is being processed by means of equipment operating automatically in response to instructions given for that purpose,

(b) is recorded with the intention that it should be processed by means of such equipment,

(c) is recorded as part of a relevant filing system or with the intention that it should form part of a relevant filing system, or

(d) does not fall within paragraph (a), (b) or (c) but forms part of an accessible record as defined by section 68.

---

[2] See paragraph 1 of the Act for all definitions quoted in this chapter and the next.

The definition of data is wide, and the 1998 Act extends the definition in the 1984 Act in four main ways.

- The 1984 Act excluded certain information held on computer; the 1998 Act makes no exceptions.
- The 1998 Act much more explicitly covers non-text data such as photographs, audio and video material, and biometric data (such as fingerprints, iris patterns or DNA samples).
- The 1984 Act did not cover paper systems; the 1998 Act does.
- The 1998 Act introduces a new category covering material intended to be put onto computer or to become part of a relevant manual system. 'Computer' is used here as shorthand for any equipment operating automatically.

What is a 'relevant filing system'?

Ever since the EU Directive came out there has been debate over which manual records are covered, and this has been the subject of considerable discussion in Parliament.

The Directive states that it should apply to manual systems only 'if the data processed are contained or are intended to be contained in a filing system structured according to specific criteria relating to individuals, so as to permit easy access to the personal data in question'.

It then goes on to define a 'personal data filing system' as 'any structured set of personal data which are accessible according to specific criteria, whether centralised, decentralised or dispersed on a functional or geographical basis'.

The definition which the UK government came up with, and the one which is in the Act (after minor amendment in Parliament) was significantly different.

Relevant filing system

means any set of information [not on a computer] relating to individuals to the extent that … the set is structured, either by reference to individuals or by reference to criteria relating to individuals, in such a way that specific information relating to a particular individual is readily accessible.

The government has clearly attempted to narrow the definition down by inserting the condition that 'specific information relating to a particular individual' must be readily accessible. In Parliament it was stated that only very limited sets of highly structured data should be caught. However, the Data Protection Commissioner expressed public disagreement with the government's interpretation, and she has indicated that she will adopt a wider definition than the government would like.[3]

---

[3] It is also possible for the Directive itself to over-ride UK law if it can be shown that the UK government has not accurately implemented the Directive.

It is probably safest to take a fairly broad view, and to treat borderline cases on the assumption that they are covered. This means that any file or set of files (or, for example, a box of index cards) where you can go easily to the information about a specific individual is quite likely to be within the Act.

Note that the information must be in a 'set'. A single phone number on a sticky note wouldn't be covered, but an alphabetical list of personal phone numbers might be.

For an indication of how this might work in practice, take the example of a complaints file where the complaints are received from individuals. Much of the content could well be highly sensitive, so one might expect Data Protection rules to apply automatically.

However, if the file is merely in date order of when each complaint was received, with no index, then it probably does not fall within the definition above, because you cannot go to the file with the intention of finding information about a specific known individual. (This does not necessarily mean that it would fall outside an organisation's confidentiality policy, of course.)

On the other hand, if the complaints are filed in alphabetical order of the person who complained, then the likelihood is that it would be covered.

There is even a third possibility: if all the complaints about each member of staff were filed together, then the set of information might be personal data about the staff members rather than about the complainants.

There is also the question as to whether all the information in a 'relevant filing system' would be covered equally by Data Protection. If a set of personnel files contained standard data on all staff – contracts, salary details, holiday records – but extensive records of disciplinary proceedings on just one member of staff, would the disciplinary record be 'specific information'?

This is such a complex area that anomalies are bound to be thrown up. Once the Act has been in place for some time, guidance from the Data Protection Commissioner, and even case law, will begin to clarify some of the issues. Meanwhile, you are unlikely to go too far off course if you take a common-sense approach to interpreting the definition and err on the side of caution.

Information intended to go onto computer or into the files

There are potentially important consequences from the inclusion as data of material intended to form part of a computer or manual record. What this means is that the forms on which you collect information come within the scope of the Act, even if you discard them as soon as the data is in your system.

Application forms, booking forms and interview notes are just some examples of what could be covered by this element of the Act.

All the responsibilities of Data Controllers – to act fairly, to ensure appropriate security, and not to keep data longer than necessary, for example (and which are discussed below) – apply with equal force to these 'data capture' documents.

The Data Subject

A Data Subject is anyone whose personal data is processed. While you may be able to identify most of your 'primary' Data Subjects without difficulty, it is worth paying attention to the inadvertent creation of 'secondary' Data Subjects. For example, if you have a personnel system, your staff will clearly be Data Subjects. However, you may well ask them for details of next of kin, or emergency contacts. If these details are put on computer, the additional people are also likely to be Data Subjects, with all the rights that this involves (as described in later chapters).

If your personnel records are in manual files the emergency contacts may not be Data Subjects because you can't 'readily' find out anything about them; you can only go by the staff member's name on the file. However, if you routinely collect information about the partners and children of staff members, there may be a case for claiming that these people could be readily located, even in manual files.

Data Subjects can also be people who have provided information about someone else. A social worker, for example, or someone who provides a reference, may be a Data Subject if their name goes onto your computer. Even if it doesn't, they generally have specific rights if the person they have provided information about wants to see their file (see Chapter 10).

Summary

Most information that voluntary organisations hold about people will be 'personal data', and therefore covered by the Act.

In the vast majority of cases there will be no dispute. Examples include:

- client or case records;
- records of staff and volunteers;
- membership records;
- newsletter mailing lists;
- fundraising or supporter databases;
- training administration records (whether for external or internal courses);
- most conference administration and bookings systems;
- contact databases (unless they contain information exclusively about organisations);

- computer-based sales records, where the purchaser's details are kept;
- lists of consultants, trainers or other resource people.

The two key questions are: is it 'personal', and is it 'data'? If the answer to both is 'yes', using the definitions above, then the set of information is covered by the Act.

EXAMPLES

① Maria runs a befriending service which uses a couple of dozen volunteers. When anyone applies to be a volunteer they fill in a form, which then gets filed. There is a separate file for each volunteer, and they are in alphabetical order. Holiday records and training records are also kept in these files. Should Maria treat the files as personal data?

She quickly realises that in this manual system she can easily find specific information about particular people, and therefore that it should be treated as personal data.

② Martin is campaigns officer for a national charity. He has a contact database of organisations working in the same field, stored on his computer. Each organisation has a named contact person. Is there personal data in the database?

Martin's conclusion is yes – even though the name of the person and their position in the organisation may be the only information held about them.

③ Rajan is surprised to see a Data Protection statement in the reception area of a big multi-national company which has donated facilities to his organisation for a conference. They use closed-circuit television (CCTV)[4] to monitor each area of the office for security purposes. Because only a small number of people work in each section, and the tapes are filed by section, their security manager has decided that the contents of the tapes may well be personal data. He can find out 'readily' whether a particular person was in their work area at a specific time. To be safe, the company publicises this prominently.

④ A telephone helpline takes a lot of details about its callers, but allows them to remain anonymous. Susan, the operations manager, transfers the information to computer so that she can analyse the pattern of calls. Is the information on computer personal data? What about the paper records of calls?

---

[4] CCTV has been the subject of one of the first draft Codes of Practice issued by the Data Protection Commissioner under the 1998 Act. The draft Code is available on the Commissioner's Web site.

Susan realises that if all the information on the computer is anonymous and there is no way of identifying the people via other information (on paper, for example), then the computer database is not personal data. The paper records might be personal data if they include the names of people who rang up and they are filed so that individual people's records can be easily found.

⑤ William is a personnel manager in a large charity. He gets a lot of people writing in asking about employment. They are each sent a personalised, word-processed letter, and their enquiry is put in a big file called 'Employment Enquiries'. When a vacancy comes up, someone looks through the file and sends the details of the job to anyone who looks suitable. William wonders whether the 'employment enquiries' file might be personal data? And what about the word-processed reply letters?

Eventually William decides that the 'employment enquiries' file is not personal data. Technically, he thinks that the word-processed letters could be personal data, even if the personalised letter is not saved. (In practice, however, he realises that the consequences of the letters being personal data are likely to be minimal.)

2

Who is the Data Controller?

The concept of the Data Controller is an important element in the 1998 Act. If you are a Data Controller, the Act applies to you. If you are not a Data Controller, your responsibilities are more limited. You need to work out, therefore, whether you are a Data Controller (or, more likely, whether the organisation you work for is a Data Controller).

The definition appears, at first sight, quite straightforward. The Data Controller is whoever decides why and how personal data is to be processed.

> **Data Controller**
>
> means ... a person who (either alone or jointly or in common with other persons) determines the purposes for which and the manner in which any personal data are, or are to be, processed;

The first point to note is that the definition uses the word 'person', not 'individual'. In other words, a legal 'person' – such as a limited company – can be a Data Controller. An 'unincorporated' organisation is not a legal person,[5] which would appear to mean that such an organisation cannot then be the Data Controller.

However, the practice under the 1984 Act has been to allow unincorporated associations to register in the name of the organisation, rather than under its trustees. The Data Protection Commissioner has indicated that this approach is likely to continue, with the Commissioner happy to treat the organisation itself as the Data Controller. Whether this will be the final position on this remains to be seen. The view favoured by many lawyers is that each individual on the Management Committee or Board of Trustees may technically be a Data Controller, acting 'jointly' with the others.

For most day-to-day purposes you can probably behave as though an unincorporated organisation was in fact the Data Controller. However, it is as well that your Committee or Trustees are made aware of the precise situation. If in any doubt about what this means, you should take qualified legal advice.

---

[5] Don't forget that whether your organisation is incorporated or not has nothing to do with whether it is a charity or not. It could be both incorporated and a charity, or one and not the other, or neither. See Appendix A for a note on this issue.

Joint activities and consortia

There are likely to be situations where two organisations, acting jointly or in common, are Data Controllers of the same personal data. For example, you may be organising a conference in collaboration with another organisation, deciding together on the 'purposes' for which the personal data is collected and the 'manner' in which it is processed. Both organisations may well have responsibilities as Data Controllers.

There are also situations in which several organisations get together in a formal consortium and agree to share client data, so that a person known to one organisation in the consortium does not have to provide their details all over again when they approach another. Here it is likely that the organisations would each be Data Controllers, acting in common – but they could end up carrying some of the responsibility if another member of the consortium breached the Act. It would be advisable in such a situation to clarify in writing both the conditions under which data would be shared, and the respective Data Protection responsibilities each member of the consortium undertakes.[6]

When might an individual be a Data Controller?

An individual employee is never likely to be the Data Controller of personal data which is used by an organisation in the course of its activities. The Data Controller will be either the organisation itself or the people who carry the final responsibility. The staff member will merely be an 'agent' of the Data Controller.

However, the case may be less clear when it comes to volunteers or to self-employed people who carry out a particular service for the organisation. Although the Act says that an 'employee' is not a Data Controller, members of the Data Protection Commissioner's staff have indicated that they believe this applies to volunteers as well, even though they are technically not employees. You would, however, have to look carefully at who actually made the decisions and took responsibility for the data in order to decide who is the Data Controller.

Note that the Act does not apply to genuine domestic use.[7] Someone using a home computer to maintain their Christmas-card list is totally exempt. This exemption does not apply, however, if you handle personal data at home on behalf of an organisation, even a small, informal, voluntary one with no money and no staff. Even holding a card index recording the birthdays of children who attend your local playgroup could make you a Data Controller. (The Data Controller might be the playgroup if it had asked you to do this.)

---

[6] The Data Protection Commissioner has issued specific guidance on the issues raised by information-sharing protocols under the 1998 Crime and Disorder Act. Although voluntary organisations do not have specific responsibilities under this Act, many are concerned with its practical application and may therefore be interested in the guidance.

[7] See also chapter 15.

Where there is a serious possibility of confusion, it is likely to be worth establishing the situation very clearly on paper – possibly through your contract if you are paying people for services. Again, qualified legal advice is strongly recommended.

Even where individuals are clearly not Data Controllers, many organisations will wish to identify a specific staff member as Data Protection Compliance Officer. This person will have a clear responsibility to be informed about Data Protection issues, to ensure that the organisation complies with its obligations, and to train or brief other staff in what they are allowed to do, what they are not allowed to do, and what to do if they are in any doubt.

Data Processors

Instead of, or even as well as, being a Data Controller, an organisation may be a Data Processor. This is defined in the Act.

Data Processor

... means any person (other than an employee of the Data Controller) who processes the data on behalf of the Data Controller;

The Act goes on to lay down conditions applying to a Data Processor. The key points are as follows.

- The Data Processor must be following directions from the Data Controller. If they have any discretion at all, the chances are that the organisation is not a Data Processor but a Data Controller in its own right.
- There must be a written contract between the Data Controller and the Data Processor.
- The Data Processor has a specific duty to take adequate security measures (see Chapter 11).
- The Data Controller has a responsibility to check that the Data Processor's security is appropriate.

In some cases where two organisations share data it may not be easy to distinguish between several possible relationships.

- They might be joint Data Controllers of a common set of data.
- One organisation might be the Data Controller, with another acting as a Data Processor.
- One organisation might be the Data Controller, making regular disclosures of information to the other. The recipient organisation may or may not be a Data Controller in its own right, depending on the form in which the data is disclosed and the way it is subsequently handled.

Summary

- Most organisations will be Data Controllers, or can behave as though they are.
- Individuals are unlikely to be Data Controllers in their role as employees, although in other circumstances an individual can certainly be a Data Controller.
- An organisation may need to identify a member of staff as Data Protection Compliance Officer.
- Where two or more organisations share data closely, they need to be particularly careful to identify their respective Data Protection responsibilities clearly, and in many cases will find it best to state them in writing.

EXAMPLES

⑥ Harry and Sally are outreach workers from two different drugs organisations. They decide to organise a one-off conference for colleagues in the sector. Between them they work out: what information to collect on the booking form, whether to send people confirmation slips when they book, which details are included in the participants' list available at the conference, and so on. Because Sally has a better computer, they decide that she will actually set up and manage the database where the participants' details are kept.

They do not set up a separate organisation to run the conference, but they agree that both organisations are likely to be Data Controllers with respect to the data they collect. Luckily, both organisations have already notified training and conference administration as a purpose they undertake, and there is no need to update their notification entries.

Because Sally is running the database, they decide to base their Data Protection policy on her organisation's approach and, in particular, to adopt her security policy. Their materials, where relevant, have to identify both organisations as Data Controllers.

⑦ Brian is a keen member of his local church. Without consulting anyone, he plans to build up a small database on his home computer of people who are likely to help with the annual Christmas Fair. Just in time, he realises that this will make him a Data Controller. He decides it would be better if the church were the Data Controller, so hands over control before starting the project.

⑧ A mediation service uses self-employed sessional mediators. The case notes are recorded by the counsellors and kept by them. The service knows which clients are on which counsellor's case-list, but holds no further details. The service has strict rules on confidentiality but makes no other rules about what information should be recorded or how it should be kept. This raises the possibility of each individual counsellor being the Data Controller for the information they hold (depending on how they hold it). After consultation, the organisation decides that it would be better to issue clear instructions to the counsellors about what to hold and how, including rules on security and confidentiality, to make it clear that the organisation is the Data Controller.

⑨ Veronica is in charge of fundraising at a large charity. In addition to mailing their previous donors, they have a contract with a specialist telephone fundraising agency which calls people to ask for money. Because there is a written contract, and because this makes it clear that it is the charity which makes all the decisions, then the fundraising agency is a Data Processor, with the charity remaining the Data Controller at all times.

However, Veronica has also developed a small 'Friends of the Millennium Project' group of volunteers. She gives them the names and details of the 500 top donors and says, in effect, 'Raise as much money from these people as you can, in whatever way you think best.' Unless she makes this relationship more formal, she realises that in this case the group of volunteers would almost certainly be a Data Controller in its own right.

⑩ Half a dozen projects in an inner-city area get together to pool their services. Through a Lottery grant they are able to set up a big client database which they all have access to. The idea is that anyone coming into contact with any of the participating organisations only has to go through one registration process. After that they can just turn up to use any of the services.

The Steering Committee for the project realises that there is a complex situation here. Can all the organisations be equally trusted to take good care of the client data? How will the clients feel about their information being shared? They decide that only a clear written policy will do, setting out:

- each organisation's responsibilities as a Data Controller;
- the security measures they will undertake;
- the protocols under which shared data can be used within each organisation.

In addition, the Steering Committee makes sure that the design of the database has strong security precautions built in – for example, so that people can normally see only the basic registration details of each client. If they need to see anything more sensitive they need authorisation, a good reason, and a strictly controlled password.

3

The Data Protection Principles

At the heart of the 1998 Act is the list of eight Data Protection Principles. Although the 1984 Act also has eight Principles, many of which are similar, there are crucial differences. The most important change is that the Data Protection Principles now apply to *all* Data Controllers. Under the 1984 Act, they applied only to those who had to register. Even a Data Controller that only processes manual data is now bound by the Principles.

The Data Protection Principles[8]

1   Personal data shall be processed fairly and lawfully and, in particular, shall not be processed unless –
    (**a**) at least one of the conditions in Schedule 2[9] is met, and
    (**b**) in the case of sensitive personal data, at least one of the conditions in Schedule 3 is also met.

2   Personal data shall be obtained only for one or more specified and lawful purposes, and shall not be further processed in any manner incompatible with that purpose or those purposes.

3   Personal data shall be adequate, relevant and not excessive in relation to the purpose or purposes for which they are processed.

4   Personal data shall be accurate and, where necessary, kept up to date.

5   Personal data processed for any purpose or purposes shall not be kept for longer than is necessary for that purpose or those purposes.

6   Personal data shall be processed in accordance with the rights of data subjects under this Act.

7   Appropriate technical and organisational measures shall be taken against unauthorised or unlawful processing of personal data and against accidental loss or destruction of, or damage to, personal data.

8   Personal data shall not be transferred to a country or territory outside the European Economic Area unless that country or territory ensures an adequate level of protection for the rights and freedoms of data subjects in relation to the processing of personal data.

---

[8]   Schedule 1, Part I of the Act.
[9]   See the following chapter for more about Schedules 2 and 3.

Principle 1 concerns 'fair' processing, and sets out in some detail actions that Data Controllers must take, as well as conditions they must meet, in order for processing to avoid being unfair. Unfortunately, it cannot be fully understood without reference to Schedules 2 and 3 of the Act (Schedule 1 covers the Principles themselves). Unlike the Data Protection Principles in the 1984 Act, therefore, the new ones don't lend themselves so easily to being used for briefing staff on how to work within the Act. Some ideas on how to present the new Act to staff and volunteers are given in Chapter 16.

Principle 2 is less specific than its equivalent in the 1984 Act. Previously, the rule was simple because it was based on registration: you had to register what you were going to do and then you could only use data for the purpose(s) that you had registered.

Under the 1998 Act the Data Controller still has to have a 'specified' purpose or purposes, but they may not have to notify the Data Protection Commissioner (the new equivalent of registration). This means that notification is now just one way in which you can specify a purpose. The other, if you are not required to notify, is to specify the purpose directly to the Data Subject.

The 'purposes' defined for the 1998 Act are generally broader than those for the 1984 Act, and a single purpose can encompass a wide range of activities. Examples of purposes include:[10]

- **Staff administration**: appointments or removals, pay discipline, superannuation, work management or other personnel matters in relation to the staff of the Data Controller.
- **Consultancy and advisory services**: giving advice or rendering professional services. The provision of services of an advisory, consultancy or intermediary nature. You will be asked to indicate the nature of the services which you provide.
- **Fundraising** in support of your objectives.
- **Processing for not-for-profit organisations**: establishing or maintaining membership of or support for a body or association which is not established or conducted for profit, or providing or administering activities for individuals who are either members of the body or association or have regular contact with it.
- **Realising the objectives of a charitable organisation or voluntary body**: the provision of goods or services in order to realise the objectives of the charity or voluntary body.

Principles 3, 4 and 5 are very similar to their equivalents in the 1984 Act, and essentially insist that data should be of good quality. While there may be specific cases in which it is hard to draw a clear line, most Data Controllers would in any case want to follow these principles.

---

[10]   These are taken from the Data Protection Commissioner's *Notification Handbook: a complete guide to notification.*

For how long is it 'necessary' to keep data?

There is no simple rule for deciding when to destroy, erase or archive data, because it all depends on what is *necessary* for the purpose(s) for which it is being held. The following questions may be useful here.

- Is there a legal time limit for holding this data? For example, occupational health and safety records now have to be held for 40 years. Information on employment selection must be held for the six months within which an unsuccessful candidate would have the right to bring a claim of discrimination.
- Do you have specific advice from professionals? For instance, your professional indemnity insurer may want you to keep detailed client records for as long as a negligence claim might be valid.
- Has the reason for holding the data changed? When a member of staff leaves, it might be the appropriate time to reduce their file to just those items which need permanent archiving.
- Do you know for a fact that the information is out of date? If your outgoing mail gets returned, you would have a hard job justifying keeping an address that you know is wrong.
- Does the data get used according to a routine rhythm? If you mail people to ask for money twice a year you may want to set a specific number of non-responses after which you will assume that they have lost interest.
- Can you confidently describe the next occasion on which you are going to use the data? If not, it may no longer be necessary to keep it. Keeping information 'just in case' is not only a waste of your storage space; it is unlikely to be satisfactory Data Protection practice.

Note that it is up to the Data Controller in the first instance to decide what is 'necessary', although there may be legal considerations, especially about how long it is necessary to keep personal data (see box).

In Principles 3 and 5 the decision on whether the data meets the criteria must be taken in relation to the purpose(s) for which it is being processed.

Principle 6 covers Data Subject rights. These include the right of access to their data, now including manual files, and the right to prevent processing in certain cases – in particular where direct marketing is concerned. (For more details on this, see Chapter 9.)

Principle 7 imposes a duty to have appropriate security, again now applying to manual as well as computerised records. You may have to restrict access to files by staff or volunteers, unless they have a good reason, as well as people outside the organisation.

'Organisational' security measures could include drawing up policies and procedures and training staff to follow them. 'Technical' measures include physical access control, such as locks on doors and filing cabinets, as well as things like computer passwords and back-up procedures.

When a Data Controller 'notifies', they will have to provide certain information about their security measures.

The question of security is addressed further in Chapter 11.

Principle 8 has caused considerable disagreement between the European Union and the USA. Since the US government has specifically rejected the idea of Data Protection legislation, it appeared at one point as though data transfer between Western Europe and the USA (as well as most other countries) would be seriously hampered by this principle. The commercial ramifications would have been inestimable, and a political solution was required. See Chapter 12 for more details.

Summary

- All 'processing' of personal data must be 'fair'.
- You must collect and use personal data only for specified purposes.
- The data must be adequate, relevant and not excessive.
- The data must be accurate and up to date.
- The data must not be held longer than necessary.
- Data Subjects' rights must be respected.
- You must have appropriate security.
- Special rules apply to transfers of personal data abroad.

EXAMPLES

⑪ Nirmal's advice agency receives most of its funding from the local council, under a contract. One year, the council announces that it is changing the conditions of its contract. In order to ensure that the funds are spent only on eligible clients, it wants to inspect random case records as part of its monitoring procedure.

Nirmal and his colleagues are understandably upset at the thought that the council officers may be seeing their confidential records, and worry about the effect this might have on clients. They wonder if they can refuse on Data Protection grounds.

One issue here is whether disclosing the records to the council officers (which is certainly 'processing') is compatible with the purpose(s) for which the data was originally collected. Would the agency be breaking the second Data Protection Principle?

Nirmal looks into it and decides provisionally that the agency has a case for refusing access. If the monitoring were for quality control, it would be possible to argue that this was an integral part of providing the service, and it therefore would be compatible with the original purpose. But auditing the agency's use of funds is a separate activity. The agency therefore asks the council to reconsider, and to look for a way of monitoring that does not involve breaches of either client confidentiality or Data Protection.

⑫ Melissa runs an organisation that promotes good childcare. Over time, it has built up a database of many of the local childminders, which it uses to send out relevant information and invitations to training events. The organisation gets a lot of phone calls from people asking if they can recommend a childminder in the area, but the organisation is reluctant to do this. Instead, it considers publishing its database as a list which people could use to make their own selection.

However, Melissa points out that in her view this is a completely different purpose from the original one of providing services to the childminders. If the organisation wants to do this, she feels that it needs to go back to the people on the database and, in effect, collect the data anew for this new purpose.

⑬ A community transport organisation starts to get comments from its drivers that they need to have more information about the service users in order to provide a good service. If they knew that someone needed help getting from their door to the vehicle, for example, the drivers could get out straight away and offer the help. They argue that it is relevant to providing the service, and therefore compatible with the third Data Protection Principle. The Management Committee agrees and decides to collect this additional information from service users who are happy to give it.

The committee also decides that they need to be careful not to collect too much data. They don't actually need to know the person's specific disability, just the kind of support that they might need. So they redesign their record forms to ask very direct questions: 'Do you want the driver to come to your door to assist?' 'Can you get into the vehicle without the hoist?' 'Will you normally have a dog and/or carer with you?'

⑭ Some of the users of the Afro-Caribbean Elders Day Centre are reluctant to reveal their ages. Michael, a former volunteer worker, was embarrassed about asking this, so he used to guess when filling in the database. After a talk by the council Welfare Rights Officer, the centre realises that some of their users could be claiming age-related benefits. Joyce, the centre manager, agrees that this use of data is within the original purpose, so she agrees to search the database for users over a specific age.

The first problem is that the database has been set up to record the age of the person when they first started using the centre. These ages have not been updated, so the centre is in danger of breaking the fourth Data Protection Principle: the data is not kept up to date. For now, the staff realise that they can work out the correct ages by seeing how long the person has been a user, but for the future they decide to change the database so that it records date of birth and calculates the current age, rather than recording a specific age.

Then they find that some of the ages Michael has guessed turn out to be under-estimates. When Joyce pulls off a list of people to talk to about the benefits they may be entitled to, some of those who should be invited to the talk get missed off. These people find out that their friends are claiming a benefit that they are not, and some of them complain. This could be another breach of the fourth Data Protection Principle: the data is not accurate. Joyce decides to make it very clear to volunteers from now on that they must not guess. If they don't know the answer, they must leave the field blank or enter a specific 'don't know' value (and the database must be set up so that this is possible). In this way, if the centre is doing a similar exercise in future, the staff can make sure that those whose ages they don't know get invited to the talk as well.

Fair processing

If the Data Protection Act can be summed up in one sentence, it is probably in Principle 1: 'Personal data shall be processed fairly'. The Act goes into considerable detail about what this means.

Processing has been defined in the 1998 Act effectively to include anything that may bring you into contact with personal data: from collecting it, through holding, using, changing, copying, disclosing or passing it on, all the way through to destroying or erasing it.

Processing

… means obtaining, recording or holding the information or data or carrying out any operation or set of operations on the information or data, including:

(**a**) organisation, adaptation or alteration of the information or data,

(**b**) retrieval, consultation or use of the information or data,

(**c**) disclosure of the information or data by transmission, dissemination or otherwise making available, or

(**d**) alignment, combination, blocking, erasure or destruction of the information or data.

While all processing has to be fair, the Act is particularly concerned with how you collect or otherwise obtain personal data. In expanding on Principle 1, the Act sets out the Fair Processing Code. This spells out several things that you have to do. Without them processing is automatically unfair. But this leaves the Data Controller with a general responsibility for fairness above and beyond the specific requirements of the code.

The Code makes it clear in particular that data has not been collected fairly if:

- anyone has been deceived or misled about why it is being collected;
- the Data Subject does not know who is processing the data and what they intend to do with it.

What is 'disproportionate effort'?

Where data is obtained from a third party, the Data Subject must be told who is processing their data and why, unless it would involve 'disproportionate effort'. This is the only ground on which the information may be withheld. The Act does not define disproportionate effort, but the Data Protection Commissioner has made some limited comment on this. She will take into account:

- the cost to the Data Controller;
- the length of time it would take to provide the information;
- how easy or difficult it is to provide the information;
- the likelihood that the Data Subject already knows that the Data Controller is processing their data.

A common-sense interpretation would suggest also that the benefit of passing on the information must outweigh the cost involved (in time or money).

Thus, if you acquire details of another voluntary organisation's supporters in order to approach them for money, the effort of making sure that they know who you are and what you are doing, the first time you write, would be minimal. You should therefore tell them. You may decide that, where you hold details of emergency contact people for staff, for example, it is worth making some effort to inform them – perhaps by asking staff to get their consent before nominating them, or giving the staff member a note to pass on.

However, if your contact person in another organisation leaves and says, 'After I've left, talk to Sam if you need anything', you don't really need to go to the trouble of phoning Sam and saying 'By the way, you're now on our database as the contact for this organisation.'

There may even be cases where there is no benefit at all in informing the Data Subject. A client who tells you that their landlord is harassing them could be in serious danger if the landlord found out that they had been reported. While you must, of course, be careful to respect the individual rights of the landlord, there may well be a case for saying that the effort of telling the landlord that they are now your Data Subject was 'disproportionate' to the benefit of doing so. Note, however, that official endorsement of this approach by the Data Protection Commissioner has not been sought or given.

This does not necessarily mean that you have to go to great lengths to tell people about why you are collecting their data: it may be obvious. When you take on a new member of staff and ask them for their bank details so that you can pay them, a Data Protection statement is likely to be superfluous. You do have to take care where any intended use of the data is not immediately obvious. Even if you have specified the non-obvious purpose by notification to the Commissioner, you still have to ensure that the Data Subject knows what is going on before the processing can be fair. In particular you need to make the Data Subject aware if you intend to make any non-obvious disclosure to a third party – for example if some of the services you offer are actually delivered by someone else and you need to pass on member or client details for this to happen.

Many voluntary organisations' existing policies in areas such as client information and confidentiality will already go beyond the letter of the Data Protection requirements. However, in some cases practices may need to be changed, particularly where contact with clients is made over the telephone or through a third party acting on behalf of the organisation. The practical implications of this are discussed in Chapter 8.

Where you obtain personal data not directly from the Data Subject but from a third party, the Data Subject is still entitled to know who you are and what you are doing, unless this would require 'disproportionate effort' (see box). This means that the effort you would have to make must be compared with the benefit to the Data Subject of having the information. If you are relying on the 'disproportionate effort' exemption, you have to keep a record of your reasons.[11] You must also provide the information to anyone who asks for it. (Remember that this exemption does *not* apply to data you get from the Data Subject, only to data you obtain from someone else.)

The Secretary of State has the power to introduce special provisions for fair processing of 'general identifiers' such as National Insurance numbers, but there is no indication at the time of writing that this power is to be exercised in the foreseeable future.

Conditions for fair processing

Principle 1 refers to the 'conditions' for fair processing that are set out in Schedule 2 of the Act, and are quoted in full in the box. Data processing is not considered fair unless it meets at least one of these conditions:

1 The Data Subject has given consent.
2 Processing is necessary to carry out a contract to which the Data Subject is a party.
3 Processing is necessary to meet a legal obligation of the Data Controller.
4 Processing is necessary to protect the vital interests of the Data Subject.
5 Processing is necessary for various judicial and government functions.

---

[11] This rule has been added to the Act by Regulation (Statutory Instrument 2000 No. 185, paragraph 5).

6   Processing is in the legitimate interests of the Data Controller unless it causes harm to the Data Subject's rights, freedoms or legitimate interests.

The first condition, consent, is discussed in Chapter 6. For the other conditions, 2 to 6, the processing must be 'necessary' for the stated purpose. It is up to the Data Controller to judge in the first place what is necessary.

The Data Protection Commissioner has indicated that 'vital interests' (Condition 4) will be interpreted very narrowly, as 'life or death' emergencies. She does not want to see it used routinely. Many voluntary organisations may want to make the case that situations such as actual or potential homelessness, harassment, abuse and

---

Conditions relevant for purposes of the first principle: processing of any personal data (Schedule 2 of the Act)

1   The data subject has given his consent to the processing.

2   The processing is necessary:
   (a) for the performance of a contract to which the data subject is a party, or
   (b) for the taking of steps at the request of the data subject with a view to entering into a contract.

3   The processing is necessary for compliance with any legal obligation to which the data controller is subject, other than an obligation imposed by contract.

4   The processing is necessary in order to protect the vital interests of the data subject.

5   The processing is necessary:
   (a) for the administration of justice,
   (b) for the exercise of any functions conferred on any person by or under any enactment,
   (c) for the exercise of any functions of the Crown, a Minister of the Crown or a government department, or
   (d) for the exercise of any other functions of a public nature exercised in the public interest by any person.

6   (1) The processing is necessary for the purposes of legitimate interests pursued by the data controller or by the third party or parties to whom the data are disclosed, except where the processing is unwarranted in any particular case by reason of prejudice to the rights and freedoms or legitimate interests of the data subject.
   (2) The Secretary of State may by order specify particular circumstances in which this condition is, or is not, to be taken to be satisfied.

threats of serious violence are also 'vital interests'. As things stand, however, this is not the Data Protection Commissioner's interpretation (see also the next chapter).

While all processing has to meet at least one of the six conditions, not all instances of processing the same set of data need meet the same condition.

- Data collected with consent might subsequently be used without consent to protect the vital interests of the Data Subject, provided that this is compatible with the original purpose for which it was collected.
- Data collected in connection with a contract might be used in the interests of the Data Controller (for example if staff details were provided to an employer's liability insurer), again provided that this was compatible with the purpose(s) specified at the time when the data was obtained.
- Some people on a contact database may have given consent (by asking to be kept in touch), while others may be there on the grounds of the Data Controller's legitimate interests (for example because they are local councillors), without having consented.

It is very hard to envisage any reasonable activity in most voluntary organisations which would fail to meet at least one of the conditions. The requirement to meet the conditions is therefore unlikely to impose any major burden. The important point is that the Data Controller must be able to say, if the question is raised, which condition (or conditions) they are relying on.

Summary

All processing of personal data must meet at least one of six conditions. It must take place:

- with the consent of the Data Subject;
- in connection with a contract involving the Data Subject;
- to meet a legal obligation;
- to protect the Data Subject's 'vital interests';
- to fulfil a wide range of government functions;
- in your 'legitimate interests', provided that the Data Subject is not harmed.

EXAMPLES

⑮ The staff of a sheltered-housing scheme find that some of the residents are being bombarded with marketing material after filling in a 'lifestyle questionnaire'. They decide to help the residents complain on the grounds that they were misled about the purpose of the survey, and that the processing of their data is therefore unfair.

(16) A council for voluntary service maintains a database of local organisations, with details of contact people. The information officer, Jane, is unsure whether she can keep these contact names without consent. She is quickly reassured that this use of the data is likely to fall under Condition 6: it is in the legitimate interests of the Data Controller and the Data Subjects are not being harmed (they gave their names voluntarily as contact people, after all). However, if the CVS were in the business of publishing a directory of local organisations, it would need to consider whether those contact people who had given their home address could be included without consent. The details of the organisations themselves, of course, are not covered by Data Protection.

(17) Barry is the secretary of a small charitable trust which gives money to individuals in the locality. He keeps a list of beneficiaries on his computer and has been complying with the Data Protection Act as a Data Controller. Then his trust decides to merge with another one. The new organisation is technically a new Data Controller, but the committee decides not to contact previous beneficiaries of either trust whose records are now in the new combined archive, on the grounds of disproportionate effort.

For further examples of the Fair Processing Code in operation, see Chapter 8.

5

Processing sensitive personal data

'Sensitive' data, as defined in the Act (see box), is subject to special rules. The definition is quoted here in full and has omissions that may cause surprise. Although details of personal finances, and other data such as age or date of birth, may well be felt by some people to be highly sensitive, it is important to draw the distinction between these personal assessments and the actual requirements of the law.

> **Sensitive personal data**[12]
>
> is personal data consisting of information as to:
>
> (a) the racial or ethnic origin of the data subject,
> (b) his[13] political opinions,
> (c) his religious beliefs or other beliefs of a similar nature,
> (d) whether he is a member of a trade union (within the meaning of the Trade Union and Labour Relations (Consolidation) Act 1992),
> (e) his physical or mental health or condition,
> (f) his sexual life,
> (g) the commission or alleged commission by him of any offence, or
> (h) any proceedings for any offence committed or alleged to have been committed by him, the disposal of such proceedings or the sentence of any Court in such proceedings.

Data Protection Principle 1 states that any Data Controller processing sensitive personal data has to meet at least one of the conditions in Schedule 3. This is summarised here, and quoted in full in Appendix B. In addition to the Schedule itself, the Home Secretary has powers to extend the list of conditions. This has

---

[12] See paragraph 2 of the Act.
[13] UK legislation is not yet written in a gender-neutral way. Where the Act itself is quoted, 'he', 'him' and 'his' apply equally to women.

been done under Regulations,[14] which are taken into account in the discussion that follows.

In order to process sensitive data, you have to meet at least one of the following conditions.

1 You have the Data Subject's 'explicit' consent.
2 You have a legal obligation to process the data in connection with employment.
3 It is in the 'vital interests' of the Data Subject or another person, and either consent cannot be obtained or it is reasonable to proceed without it.
4 You are processing membership data in certain non-profit associations, but *not* most charities or voluntary organisations.
5 The data has been made public deliberately by the Data Subject.
6 You need to process the data in connection with giving legal advice or defending legal rights.
7 The processing is in connection with various judicial and government functions.
8 You need to process the data in connection with medical care and have a medical practitioner's duty of confidentiality.
9 You are processing data about ethnic or racial origin, disability or religion in order to monitor equal opportunities.
10 You need to process the data in order to provide confidential counselling, advice, support or other services, and either consent cannot be obtained or it is reasonable to proceed without it.
11 The processing is in connection with various insurance activities.

The intention is clearly that in most cases a Data Controller should aim to meet the **first condition**, which is to have the 'explicit' consent of the Data Subject. 'Explicit' is not defined, and guidance from the Data Protection Commissioner suggests only that explicit consent may need to be clearer and more detailed than the consent which may be sought for processing non-sensitive data (or, indeed, to override Principle 8 on the transfer of data overseas).

While 'explicit' consent does not have to be in writing, you may well feel it necessary to record evidence that explicit consent has been granted, either through a signature from the Data Subject or through written confirmation by the person to whom the consent was given verbally.

You can process sensitive personal data *without* the Data Subject's explicit consent only if one of the other conditions applies. In the rest of this chapter, we will look at these, and circumstances in which they might apply, one by one. If you believe that any of these conditions might apply, consult Appendix B for the full definition.

---

[14]   Statutory Instrument 2000 No. 417.

Processing sensitive data without consent

The **second condition** provides for processing which is necessary for the purposes of complying with the law in connection with employment. This would include, for example, the collection of health information in order to enable the employer to meet the requirements of the Disability Discrimination Act. (Of course you also have responsibilities towards volunteers and service users under the Disability Discrimination Act, but you could not use the second condition in these cases since they are not employees.)

The **third condition** has been the subject of much debate. It allows processing that is necessary in order to protect the vital interests of the data subject *or another person*, in cases where consent cannot be obtained or where it is reasonable to proceed without it. This is discussed further in the box.

> ## Processing in the vital interests of the Data Subject or another person
>
> Some voluntary organisations have argued that they should be able to use the third condition in order, for example, to keep a record of sex offenders who are deemed unsuitable to work with vulnerable clients. The Data Protection Commissioner apparently does not agree.
>
> This is undoubtedly sensitive data. Consent from the Data Subject (the offender) is unlikely to be an option. The vulnerable clients would fall into the category of 'another person'. So it all hinges on whether preventing the potential abuse counts as 'protecting vital interests'. It is obviously important to pay due attention to the rights of the offenders as well as the voluntary organisations' vulnerable clients, and this is not always an easy balance to strike. If you are considering using this condition to legitimise your use of sensitive data you are strongly advised to take specific advice or to consult the Data Protection Commissioner.
>
> Note also that this area will be significantly affected when the Criminal Records Agency comes into existence under the 1997 Police Act. Checks on the criminal record of prospective employees and volunteers will be available to all organisations (at different levels of completeness, depending on the work the person is seeking).[15] The use of this information will be subject to a mandatory code of practice.

The **fourth condition** allows non-profit organisations with religious, political, trade union or philosophical aims to process sensitive data about their members, or people in regular contact with the organisation, subject to certain safeguards. Verbal guidance from the Data Protection Commissioner's staff

[15]   See Appendix C.

suggests that 'philosophical' aims do not cover the activities of most charities or voluntary organisations.

The **fifth condition** covers sensitive data which the Data Subject has deliberately made public. You would not, for example, need consent to record the political affiliation of someone who had stood as a candidate for a specific party.

The **sixth condition** allows sensitive data to be processed without consent where it is necessary in connection with legal proceedings, obtaining legal advice, or establishing, exercising or defending legal rights. While an advice agency would normally have no problem getting consent from clients, this could allow data about third parties to be held without their consent in connection with a broad range of advice work.

The **seventh condition** is very similar to the equivalent condition in Schedule 2, exempting government functions from the need to obtain consent for processing sensitive data.

Equalities monitoring

There may be cases where you want to carry out equal-opportunities monitoring but feel that obtaining consent would be difficult or inappropriate. Under the Act you may carry out *most* equal-opportunities monitoring without consent.

For monitoring on grounds of *racial or ethnic origin*, *disability* or *religion* (which are all sensitive data) there is specific provision.

For monitoring on grounds of *age*, *gender* or other grounds such as where people live there is no specific provision, but since this is not sensitive data you would not need consent if you could show that it is in your legitimate interests and the Data Subject is not harmed.

For monitoring on grounds of *sexuality* or *criminal record* there is *no* special provision. Since this data is sensitive, in these cases it would be necessary to have explicit consent except in the unlikely event that one of the other conditions applied.

What this means is that your equal-opportunities monitoring form need not ask people explicitly to give consent for your use of the data, unless you are asking about their sexuality or criminal record. As long as you give Data Subjects the information they must have, and make it clear that the information they provide will be used only for monitoring, your existing form may well be suitable as it stands.

The **eighth condition** relates to processing sensitive data where it is necessary for medical purposes, but only where this is done by a health professional, or someone who owes an equivalent duty of confidentiality. 'Medical purposes' is defined quite widely, to include care as well as treatment. However, it may not apply to employers seeking medical references from potential employees. The employer may need the Data Subject's consent for this use of their medical records.

The **ninth condition** makes specific provision to permit processing of sensitive data about ethnic or racial origin where this is aimed at promoting equal opportunities. Among the **additional conditions** which have been added by Regulation are ones providing for the use of information on disability or religion for equalities monitoring. In these cases the Regulation states specifically that the information must not be used for making decisions about individuals. The resulting position on equalities monitoring is summarised in the box.

Among the other **additional conditions** is one allowing processing of sensitive data for the provision of confidential counselling, advice, support or other services, provided that certain safeguards are met. The processing must be in the 'substantial public interest', and it is only permissible if, in addition:

- consent cannot be obtained, or
- it is unreasonable to obtain consent, or
- seeking consent would jeopardise the provision of the service.

This does simplify matters in a number of tricky areas. For example, a voluntary organisation providing support to carers might well be able to hold information about the medical condition of the person being cared for without their consent (which may well be impossible or unreasonable to obtain). A counselling service might well be able to record allegations of abuse without seeking the consent of the alleged abuser.

Can sensitive data be implied?

There has been some discussion about whether you can infer anything about an individual from the fact that their details come up in a particular context. For example, if someone is the contact for the local Sikh gurdwara, does that mean you are holding information about their religious beliefs? In this case it may not matter: if they have made the information deliberately public you could probably safely use the data on the grounds of the fifth condition described above.

However, if someone is on a database to receive information about a particular medical condition and you share the database with another organisation, are you disclosing sensitive data?

A common-sense approach is probably required. If the circumstances suggest that the individual does fall into a particular category where the data would be sensitive, then treat it as such. Pay particular attention to whether you actually need the data in question, and in particular to whether you can make any disclosures in a less revealing way. Get clear consent wherever possible, or give people the option to opt out.

In some cases your judgement may be that the information cannot be taken as a definitive indication of the presence of sensitive data, and therefore that you need only comply with the standard rules.

Summary

In order to process 'sensitive' personal data, you must meet at least one of the following conditions. Your processing must:

- be with the 'explicit' consent of the Data Subject;
- be necessary to meet legal requirements in connection with employment;
- be necessary to protect the vital interests of the Data Subject or another person;
- concern the membership records of some non-profit membership associations;
- involve information deliberately publicised by the Data Subject;
- be in connection with legal advice or protecting legal rights;
- be in connection with a range of government functions;
- be necessary to provide medical care;
- concern equalities monitoring on race/ethnicity, disability or religion;
- be necessary in connection with confidential counselling, advice or support work;
- be in connection with the provision of insurance.

In most cases there are limitations to the extent to which the conditions may be fulfilled. See Appendix B for the full details.

EXAMPLES

⑱ Veronica runs the fundraising department for a small medical charity. Quite often people write in with a donation and mention in the accompanying letter that the reason they are giving the donation is because they themselves have the medical condition in question. Veronica would like to keep this information on file for when she writes back in future, and wonders whether the fifth condition in Schedule 3 might apply: has the information been made 'deliberately public' by the Data Subject, or does she need to go back and get explicit consent?

She telephones the Data Protection Commissioner's office where she is told that in their view the letter does not count as being 'public'. So if

Veronica does want to keep the information she will need to satisfy one of the other conditions. In this case that almost certainly means phoning or writing back to get explicit consent.

⑲ Maddy is the Manager of a carers' support project. Her volunteers visit carers at home, and in the course of their work pick up a lot of information about not just the carer but also the person they are caring for. Some of this information is 'sensitive', such as information about the medical condition of the person being cared for.

Maddy's approach is twofold. First she has to make sure that she records only information that she genuinely needs. She consults the volunteers and they reach an agreement about the types of information that need to go into the files, both for the organisation's own monitoring and so that volunteers can pass on to each other the information they need in order to provide the services.

Secondly, some of this information does relate to the medical condition of the person being cared for, and is therefore 'sensitive' personal data. The agency workers decide that they are able to guarantee confidentiality, and that many of the people being cared for would not be in a position to give consent. They will therefore hold this information under the 'confidential services' condition.

A colleague of Maddy's, Thomas, faces a slightly different situation. His volunteers are involved in mediation and they sometimes have to visit households where some of the residents have a history of criminal violence. For the safety of the volunteers, Thomas feels that it is essential that they are aware of situations like this and, again, that it may not be appropriate to seek consent. He decides to take advice on whether he can use the same argument as Maddy or rely on the third condition, 'protecting vital interests'.

⑳ Jason applies for a new job, and his prospective employer insists that he has a medical examination, the results of which will form part of his personnel record. Because this is not in connection with providing medical care, the employer needs Jason's consent. In practice, however, Jason realises that if he withholds consent he is unlikely to get the job.

6

Data Subject consent

'Consent' is not defined in the 1998 Data Protection Act. Guidance from the Data Protection Commissioner, based on the EU Directive from which the Act is derived, indicates that consent has to be 'freely given, specific and informed', and the Data Subject has to 'signify' their wishes.

This would mean that consent can be inferred from something the Data Subject does, but not from something they don't do. In other words, if the Data Subject knows fully what is going to be done with their data and goes ahead with providing it, they can be taken to have consented. However, if you mail people saying 'we'll keep you on our database unless you tell us otherwise' the Data Protection Commissioner's view is that you don't have consent from those who don't reply, because they haven't done anything.

The Commissioner is not necessarily right, and her guidance does not have the force of law. There is an opposing legal opinion that if, for example, you are already in contact with people it might be sufficient to invite them to consent, give them easy ways to object, but then inform them that you will assume consent if you have not heard back within a given period. You could also inform them that you will continue to process their data under the sixth Condition ('legitimate interests') unless they specifically tell you not to. This issue will undoubtedly be the subject of further debate. The discussion below adheres to the Commissioner's line, but you should be aware that you may have a case for assuming consent even from a non-response in certain circumstances.

Although the consent must be 'freely given' you are allowed to explain the direct consequences of not consenting. For example, 'Without your National Insurance number we can't find out what has happened to your benefits claim.'

Data obtained from the Data Subject

When you collect information on paper, or on an electronic form, you will often be in a position to provide all the information that the Data Subject needs in order to decide whether to give consent. It may be completely obvious from the context who will use the data being collected and what for, for example on a booking form, an order form or an application form, where the name of the organisation collecting the data will be prominent and the purpose clear. You may want to reinforce this by providing a short Data Protection statement ensuring that the Data Subject is in no doubt. If they go ahead and fill in the form, and you are happy that they know exactly what they are letting themselves in for, you can take it that you have their consent.

You may be in the same situation when people give you information face to face or over the phone. If they have initiated the contact – by visiting your agency or phoning you up – they have done something specific and, again provided you are sure that they have all the information they need, you may be able to assume consent. If the contact is trivial you may need to say nothing: they phone up to order a free brochure and you record their address merely in order to get the brochure sent out when it is published in two weeks' time. Provided you won't keep the information after that, or use it for something else, they know all they need to know.

In other cases you may need to be more specific, or even to check that you do have their consent. For example, you may need to say, 'Do you mind if we keep your details so that we can let you know if we publish any other material on the same topic?'

When the contact is the beginning of a closer relationship, such as when you take on a new client, you are likely to spend time explaining the arrangements anyway. It is particularly easy if you need them to sign something at this stage, agreeing to the service you are providing. You can build consent for your use of their data into the statement they sign.

Data not obtained from the Data Subject

Where you obtain data from a third party you are obviously not in a position to get consent from the Data Subject. Although they may originally have given the organisation that is the source of the data consent to disclose it, this is not the same as giving you consent to use it (because consent must be 'specific'). If you want their consent, you have to seek it directly.

Data you hold already

You might be holding information that you obtained a long time ago without seeking consent. Do you need to do anything? It depends on the circumstances.

If the data is used for something that involves the Data Subject in doing something, you probably don't need to take any specific action. For example, if they renew their membership annually, the fact that they return their membership renewal is likely to count as consent. Of course, you mustn't use the data for anything they wouldn't expect as a member. You would need to look at the information they were provided with when they originally signed up, or which you had sent them since.

If the data is being kept for historical purposes – old client records, for example – the main requirement is for you to be sure that you are not keeping it for longer than necessary. Provided you are satisfied on this, then it is probably in your legitimate interests to keep the data, and the Data Subject is not being harmed. If so, you do not need to seek consent.

A more complex area is the type of database where you may need to contact people infrequently, but there is no regular relationship. This could include, for example, a list of people who receive your Annual Report, or a list of people who you hope may give you money in the future (and who may have given in the past) but who are not currently active donors. If you follow the Data Protection Commissioner's guidance you cannot just write to say 'tell us if you want to come off the database'. That may be a worthwhile action in its own right, but it does not solve your problem because a non-response would *not count* as consent according to the Commissioner.

The first consideration here is to make sure that everyone on the database knows that you are holding their data and why. If the names are just sitting there and not being used there is a risk that you are holding them longer than necessary. If you are not using the information, why are you holding it? If, however, you decide that you do have a legitimate interest in continuing to hold the data, then you do not necessarily need consent (for example, if you are planning a centenary appeal to all your old members in a few years' time). In any case, it is worth making sure that you do contact everyone on the list at some stage to ensure that they know you have the data, and to tell them how to get taken off your database if this is what they want.

'Explicit' consent for sensitive data

When you need explicit consent, you cannot assume that you have it merely from the fact that someone goes ahead with providing information. You need to spell out why you need the data and how you will use it, including any safeguards that you will apply, and any self-imposed restrictions on disclosures (such as not making any disclosure without the Data Subject's consent). The Data Subject then has to say, in effect, 'Knowing all that, I agree to this use of the data.'

The ideal situation is one where the Data Subject is providing information on a paper form and is signing a statement anyway. Applicants for a job may be undertaking that the statements they have given on the form are true. New clients may be asking you to take on a particular piece of work, and possibly giving you permission to act for them. Parents may be authorising you to take their children on outings or to administer medicine in emergencies. In any of these cases it is relatively easy to add a sentence to the statement they sign, inviting the person to give explicit consent for any processing of sensitive data.

The same principles could be applied to an electronic form, with appropriate safeguards to verify the identity of the individual.

Since explicit consent need not be in writing, however, there will be occasions when it is most appropriate to get the consent verbally. There is nothing wrong with this; but what if you need evidence in the future that consent had been obtained? Without a signature, the best alternative is a record made *at the time the consent is given* by the person (most likely one of your staff or volunteers) to whom the consent was given.

There are also management issues in making sure that the procedures for getting consent verbally are adhered to:

- You may need to design your forms specifically to prompt your workers to obtain explicit consent and to record the fact that they have done so.
- On screen, the consent box could be a mandatory field with no default – in other words, anyone filling in the form on screen cannot proceed without actively entering something in the field.
- From time to time you should check that the forms, on paper or screen, are being properly filled in.
- If you monitor telephone conversations for quality of service, proper consent would be one issue to look at.
- You may want to check with a sample of clients that their consent was actively sought.
- At the very least you must make sure that any staff and volunteers who might be in a position where they need to obtain consent are properly briefed on its importance and trained in how to do it.

If you are able to show that you have taken adequate steps to set up a procedure and ensure that it is followed, this would be additional support for you against any claim that you went ahead without proper consent.

Can one person consent on behalf of another?

For Data Protection purposes one person cannot consent on behalf of another unless they have a legal right to do so. In England or Wales the question of whether or not a person can give consent in their own right is a factual one: are they capable of understanding the issue sufficiently? In Scotland, children are presumed capable of giving consent from the age of 12.

Where someone is too young to give consent, only the parents – or someone with a parent's legal rights – can do so on their behalf. An adult who is incapable of giving consent can only have consent given on their behalf by someone with a power of attorney. In many cases where adults are unable to give consent, it may be better to see whether you can satisfy one of the conditions for processing that do not require consent.

Consent is not necessarily universal or permanent

The Data Protection Commissioner has expressed the view that the Data Subject may be entitled to consent to some of the things you want to do with their data but at the same time to withhold consent from others. For example, if they need to provide you with information in order to receive a service they are likely to consent to that. But if you also intend to use the information for other purposes you may need to get consent for these separately. In particular you may need specific consent for disclosing data to someone else if this is not connected with the main purpose for which the information is being obtained by you.

Because consent must be 'freely given' you would not be able to say, 'We will provide our main service only on condition that you give consent for us to use the information that we collect for a secondary purpose as well.'

Data Subjects may also withdraw consent. If you are relying on consent for meeting the fair processing conditions (in Schedule 2) and the Data Subject then decides to withdraw their consent, it would quite possibly be unfair to carry on using the data under one of the other conditions, even if you could genuinely meet one or more of them.

Summary

- Consent to use personal data must be specific, informed and freely given.
- Consent need not be in writing.
- Consent can normally be implied from something the Data Subject does, but not from anything they fail to do.
- 'Explicit' consent for processing sensitive data cannot be implied, and must be deliberately given.

EXAMPLE

㉑ Miles runs a membership organisation. Every year members get a letter asking them to renew their subscription. He decides to include on the letter a statement that members' data will be used only for administering member activities and benefits. He reasons that if members go ahead and send the form back, they have consented to this use of their data.

However, someone on the committee then proposes publishing a county-by-county list of members, so that they can get in touch with each other. Before the plan is put into action, Miles points out that this is a new venture; people may not have realised that it would be one of the member services to be undertaken, so they cannot be said to have consented to it.

The whole project is shelved until members can be asked, both in principle at the AGM and individually, whether they want their details made public in this way.

For examples of how consent might be obtained, see Chapter 8.

7

Restrictions on direct marketing

For the first time in the UK, the Act gives individuals the right to prevent the use of their data for direct marketing. This is a significant new right, and should enable people to stem, or at least reduce, the flow of 'junk mail' where they wish to. Organisations that have not already adopted good practice in allowing people to opt out of direct marketing will have to make considerable changes. The regulations also apply to charity fundraising.

What is direct marketing?

The definition of direct marketing in the Act is broad. It is 'the communication (by whatever means) of any advertising or marketing material which is directed to particular individuals'. This includes approaches for the purposes of fundraising or soliciting support (such as asking if someone would be willing to do voluntary work in a charity shop), as well as the more obvious marketing of goods or publications, distribution of a mail-order catalogue, or promotion of services such as training or other events.

Restrictions on direct marketing clearly apply to any form of contact, including (but not limited to) mail, phone calls, faxes and e-mail.

The material has to be directed to the individual. This means that it generally would *not* include:

- a flyer or brochure inserted in every copy of a magazine or other mailing;
- advertisements within publications or on posters;
- marketing material sent to an organisation.

However, it might well cover:

- marketing material sent to individuals within an organisation because of something specific you know about them (such as offering to sell a book to people who had been on a related training course);

- advertisements on a Web site if these were chosen in response to the previous browsing behaviour of the individual (assuming that the system collected enough information about the person to constitute personal data).

The right to opt out of direct marketing

The Act provides that the Data Subject may 'require' the Data Controller in writing not to use their data for direct marketing. However, you cannot leave it entirely up to the Data Subject to take the initiative, because of your responsibility to be 'fair' when obtaining information.

If you are obtaining the information directly from the Data Subject, in order to be fair you should give them the opportunity to opt out there and then, preferably through having a box to tick if they don't want future contact (an 'opt-out box'). It is much less likely to be fair if you tell them that they have to write to a separate address in order to opt out.

If you obtain the information from someone else, you need to make it clear as soon as you use the information (which in most cases will mean when you first contact the Data Subjects) that you are using it for direct marketing, and giving them the opportunity to opt out, or telling them how to opt out. Again, anything that puts unnecessary obstacles in their way (such as a premium-rate opt-out phone number) could well be unfair.

It would certainly be a contravention of the Act to use material for direct marketing if this was not one of your 'specified' purposes when you collected it.

The opt-out applies only where the material is unsolicited. If you advertise something in your newsletter and someone phones up to ask for more information, you can send a brochure even if they are marked on your database for 'no direct marketing'.

Approaching someone who has given money in the past to ask for another donation counts as unsolicited direct marketing, but following up a specific transaction is not. If someone sends a donation without giving authorisation for you to reclaim the tax under Gift Aid, or if they forget to sign their donation cheque, there is nothing to stop you getting back to them on that specific point, even if they have opted out of direct marketing.

The Telecommunications (Data Protection and Privacy) Regulations 1999

A separate piece of legislation, the Telecommunications (Data Protection and Privacy) Regulations 1999,[16] gives additional rights with respect to marketing

---

[16]   Statutory Instrument 1999 No. 2093.

carried out by telephone. These Regulations are also enforced by the Data Protection Commissioner.

The Regulations allow an individual[17] subscriber to 'notify' a caller that they don't want any further telemarketing calls from them. This 'notification' does not have to be in writing. Essentially you can tell anyone who rings with a marketing call 'Don't call again', and that should be sufficient. The definition of marketing is essentially the same as in the Data Protection Act.

The Regulations also put the Telephone Preference Service (TPS) on a statutory basis. Any individual subscriber can (in theory) prevent unwanted marketing calls by registering their phone number. Before any person or organisation makes a marketing call they must check the number they intend to ring against the register. If the number is on the register, direct marketing calls must not be made to it. It doesn't matter whether the number is from your own database, from someone else's list or from the phone book.

The register can be checked in a number of ways. Individual numbers can be checked one by one on the TPS Web site or on a premium-rate phone line. The national register, or sub-sets of it, may also be obtained in electronic format for a fee. (See **Further information** at the end of this book for details.)

The only way to make marketing calls without checking the register is if you already have permission for this from the person you are calling. For practical reasons, it is likely that consent for marketing calls would continue in operation, even if the subscriber subsequently put their number on the register. It may be worth pointing this out to people when seeking their consent for telemarketing.

A phone number can be added to the register by phone. The number to call, at the time of writing, is 0845 070 0707. Information is also available from the operator and is given near the front of up-to-date telephone directories.

The Regulations also forbid sending unsolicited faxes to individuals' lines unless they have given permission in advance. Businesses can prevent unwanted marketing faxes by registering with the Fax Preference Service which operates on similar lines to the Telephone Preference Service.

Practical implications

It is important that, if you make any use of direct marketing, your system is able to record who has consented or objected to what. The system must be reliably able to 'suppress' any individual's details if they have opted out. While a manual system may suffice for small numbers, an automatic system is likely to be more accurate.

---

[17] 'Individual' in this connection includes not only phone lines held in the name of individuals, but also those held in the name of unincorporated voluntary organisations and businesses, such as law firms, accountancy firms, surveyors, etc.

When someone does opt out, deleting them altogether from your database may be unwise. If you ever came across their name again, you would have no record that they had exercised their direct marketing opt-out and you may inadvertently end up marketing to them again, against their wishes.

You must also ensure that if you transfer information to other organisations for marketing purposes, either you exclude anyone who has opted out of direct marketing, or you include their opt-out status with the information transferred. If you obtain information from other organisations you need guarantees that they have excluded (or marked) those who have opted out of direct marketing.

Finally, it is important that all your staff and volunteers who may be in contact with Data Subjects understand the full implications of these new rights. There must be a clear procedure for acting on the wishes of anyone who says 'Stop sending me this stuff' or 'Stop phoning me'.

Summary

Who	Can object to	Who to	How	Under
Data Subject	All unsolicited direct marketing from one organisation	Data Controller	'Require in writing'	1998 Data Protection Act
Phone subscriber	Unsolicited telemarketing from one organisation	Caller	'Notify'	Telecom. 1999 Regulations
Phone subscriber	Unsolicited telemarketing from any organisation	TPS	'Notify'	Telecom. 1999 Regulations

8

Providing the Data Subject with information

A balance has to be struck between the clear requirement to ensure that a data subject has the information they are entitled to, and the danger of overloading people with unhelpful detail. This is particularly true if your initial contact with people is while they are under stress, or if there are other reasons why they may not be capable of taking in the implications of a Data Protection statement.

The rule of thumb is to ask: 'Have we done enough to ensure that the Data Subject is unlikely to get any surprises from our use of the data (including any disclosure we might make to other people) at any stage?'

As described in Chapter 4, there is certain basic information that all Data Subjects must have. Consider a standard short statement on your forms and leaflets, a standard paragraph in letters welcoming new members or clients, or a notice in your waiting room.

Data Protection statements

When you are inserting a Data Protection statement in any document, the following checklist covers some of the main considerations.

- Use the Commissioner's logo to draw attention to the statement (see box).
- Say who you are and what you are doing.
- Identify possible disclosures or transfers abroad.
- Offer an opt-out from disclosure to other organisations if this is appropriate, or explain the circumstances in which disclosure will happen.
- Offer an opt-out from direct marketing, if relevant.
- Get 'explicit' consent if required.
- Be 'fair'. Provide as much information as necessary about how you will use the data, including any security measures or self-imposed restrictions that may reassure the Data Subject.

This 'signpost' has been introduced by the Data Protection Commissioner to offer a consistent and recognisable way of drawing attention to written Data Protection statements. For more information (and an option to download the image itself) see the Data Protection Commissioner's Web site. The signpost and its intended uses are also described in a leaflet available from the Commissioner.

The following example of a Data Protection statement was issued by the Co-operative Bank plc in a newsletter to existing customers in April 2000.[18] It is an excellent example of how clear, relevant and useful information can be provided within a regular communication, and without going too far into the technicalities of the Act.

Data Protection: extending your rights

The new 1998 Data Protection Act defines your rights as an individual in relation to the information held about you, and how it may be used.

Like any bank, we hold information about our customers – ranging from names and address to the details of regular monthly expenditure.

Of course, the most important way in which we use data is in providing you with the financial service you have requested. But since, in some circumstances, we may pass on information about you, with your consent – for example, to a credit reference agency – it's absolutely essential that you should trust us to act responsibly, and in your interests.

Our undertaking, your rights

We fully accept this responsibility and are happy to give you a firm undertaking that we will keep information about you up-to-date and accurate, and do everything we can to prevent it from being used in any unauthorised or unlawful way.

In addition to our commitment, the new Data Protection Act gives you more extensive rights in relation to the information we hold about you.

If you prefer that we stop using your information for the purpose of advising you about our services, or if you feel that we are using information about you in any way which you believe may cause you (or another person) substantial damage or distress, you can write to us at the address below to request that your records are no longer used in this way.

---

[18] Quoted here with permission.

However, we hope that you trust us to respect your interests and the information we have about you.

We also hope you have found that The Co-operative Bank places a very high value on trust and openness. If you feel you would like to know more about how we are complying with the new Data Protection Act, please write to Customer Care, Delf House, Southway, Skelmersdale, Lancashire, WN8 6NY. If you would like us to send you a copy of the information we hold about you, please write to the same address specifying your account number and enclosing a cheque for £10 payable to 'The Co-operative Bank plc'.

Data Protection and the Web

In some ways, information collected over the Internet requires more care, and the Data Subjects require more reassurance, than in more traditional settings. If you are based in the UK, or if any of the personal data you use is processed in the UK, then UK Data Protection law applies, even if your Data Subjects are on the other side of the world.

Unless your Web site is merely used for publishing, and doesn't collect any feedback or information from users (with or without their knowledge), you will need a Data Protection and Privacy statement. Some of the information in it will be similar to the information you have to provide on printed material, but other aspects are specific to the Internet. The statement should contain information on the following points;[19]

- who is collecting the data;
- what personal data is being collected, both overtly and covertly;
- what the purpose of the collection is;
- how long the data will be kept;
- where the data might be transferred to;
- what rights the consumer has with respect to the data (for example access, correction and deletion) and how they can be exercised;
- how the consumer can decline e-mail advertising;
- who should be contacted for more information;
- what security measures are in place, especially where the consumer is being asked to part with information like credit-card details;
- whether anonymous browsing is possible;
- the policy on cookies and IP addresses;[20]
- whether responsibility is declined for the privacy practices on linked sites;
- obtaining the consumer's consent or agreement to the use of their data.

---

[19] This section, including the model privacy statement, is based on material written by Angus Hamilton, a solicitor whose firm specialises in Data Protection, Internet regulation, computers and the law and litigation, and first published in PC Pro. For more information see www.btinternet.com/~hamiltons/. The material is quoted here with permission.

The statement should be:

- positioned prominently;
- linked into all pages that gather data;
- adapted for use in different jurisdictions according to different local laws;
- reviewed and updated regularly;
- complied with.

Model privacy statement

ABC Ltd doesn't capture and store any personal information about individuals who access this Web site, except where you voluntarily choose to give us your personal details via e-mail or by enquiring about or ordering any of our services.

In these latter cases, the personal information you give us is used exclusively by ABC for providing you with current and future information about our products and services and any other services described in this Web site. We don't pass any of your personal data to outside organisations and/or individuals, except with your express consent.

ABC doesn't send cookies from this site, and only monitors the IP address of visitors to assess which pages are the most popular. These IP addresses aren't linked to any personal data so that visitors to our site remain anonymous.

You have a right to know about the personal information ABC Ltd holds about you. You also have a right to have your data corrected or deleted. Please address all your requests and/or queries about our Data Protection policy to ABC Ltd at our UK office address.

Don't forget, also, that it is accepted good practice to ensure that you include a 'real world' postal address and possibly telephone number on all Web sites, so that users know where to find you and have an alternative means of contacting you or checking your *bona fides*.

Disproportionate effort

As discussed in Chapter 4 above, you do not have to provide the Data Subject with information if it would involve 'disproportionate effort'. This does not mean that you can just decide that it would be too much bother. You must be able to justify this.

You can certainly reduce the effort in many cases. Could you put a notice in your waiting room? You may decide that you don't then need to say anything further in your discussions with clients, service users or visitors. Could you include the information in something you are sending people anyway – a short statement in your newsletter, for example?

---

[20] In other words, whether the Web site will collect information about the user in ways they may not be aware of.

You could also make a point of telling people how to find out more if they want to. Prepare a more detailed statement about your activities which is ready for anyone who asks.

Data about third parties

A complication may arise where you collect information about a third party (perhaps another family member, a landlord, or someone the Data Subject is in dispute with) at the same time as getting other information from the Data Subject. In some circumstances, particularly if the information is put on computer, the third party may also be a Data Subject. Do they have to be informed of this, and if so, how?

Where you are fairly sure that the third party is happy with the situation, you are likely to want them to know what is happening. For example, if someone is down as the emergency contact for a child in your care, you have an interest in checking that they know this and have agreed. Otherwise they may not be available when you need them. One way to inform them would be to contact them yourself. Alternatively, when you collect the information from the Data Subject you could perhaps get them to confirm that they have told the person that their name is being put down, and possibly that they have given their consent.

Do remember that the consent must genuinely come from the person themselves. Your 'primary' Data Subject can't normally consent on someone else's behalf.

There may be other cases where you don't want the third party to know you have information about them. Normally you have no option but to inform them. However, see 'disproportionate effort' above and on page 19.

Template for an information panel

It is important not to go overboard in providing information. The example overleaf is not intended to be a model to be used in full. Rather it is a template, where all the parts in round brackets '( )' have to be filled in with your own information, while the parts in square brackets '[ ]' are optional, to be used only if they apply.

The words can, of course, be adapted to suit your particular audience.

We/(The Data Controller) will use the information you have provided here [, and other information you may provide us with in the future] for the purpose[s] of (purposes).

[We will not disclose this information to any other person or organisation, except in connection with the above purposes. / We may disclose this information to other [type of] organisations for the purpose of (purpose). If you object to such disclosure, please tick here ☐.]

[Other information required to make the collection fair.]

[If you do not want us to contact you about other [products/services/ projects/events/etc] in future, please tick this box ☐.]

[We may contact you in future by telephone about other [products/ services/projects/events/etc]. If you object, please tick this box ☐.]

If you have any query about the use we make of your data, please contact (Data Protection Officer).

[With respect to the data about (sensitive areas) we will (details). Please sign here to show that you agree to us using your data in this way.

I agree to the above use of my data. Signed:]

Summary

- When you provide information to the Data Subject, make sure that it is prominent, easily identified and easily understood.
- Don't provide so much information that people are overwhelmed, but tell them how to get more details if they wish.
- Put appropriate information in appropriate places – your newsletter, forms that people complete, or your Web site all need a different approach.
- Remember to ensure that you inform people whose data you get from someone else, unless it involves 'disproportionate effort'.

EXAMPLES

㉒ Vince runs a training programme. When organisations book people onto courses they obviously have to provide personal data about the participants. Vince thinks about what he does with the data and decides that he is confident that the Data Subjects know enough about what is going on. His organisation's name is prominent on the booking form, and he uses the information only for administering the training course and making sure everyone pays. The names of delegates are put on the computer, so they are personal data, but he decides not to put a Data Protection statement on the form.

However, the next time he runs a course he finds himself routinely printing off a list of participants and faxing it to the course tutor. He also normally puts a copy of the participants' list into the course packs. On reflection he decides that this may still be OK: he's only doing what people might expect; but he wants to be on the safe side. So he does add a short statement to his booking form explaining that the names and organisations, only, of the participants will be disclosed to the tutor in advance and to other participants.

The next development is that instead of marketing future courses to the participants' organisations, Vince decides to identify courses that people might be interested in and write directly to them. Because this is direct marketing directed to the individual, he now needs to make this clear on the form, and to offer an opt-out box.

He also decides that the information he collects about special needs should have the Data Subject's explicit consent.

Vince ends up with a statement which says:

Information you provide in connection with our training courses will not be disclosed outside our organisation, except where necessary in order to facilitate the training. All participants are given a list of participants' names and organisations, but no further details.

If you do not want us to contact you in future about other training courses, events or publications, please tick this box □.

With respect to the details of your special needs, please sign here to indicate that you consent to our use of this data in order to make your participation as rewarding as possible, including disclosing the information to the trainer.

I agree to the above use of my data. Signed:

㉓ The Data Protection and confidentiality poster in an advice agency reads:

This agency has a strict policy on confidentiality and we aim to take good care of any information we have about you. If you want to know more, please ask any of our advisers to explain or to give you a leaflet.

㉔ The clause at the bottom of a job application form could read:

All the information I have given here is true. I consent to the use of all this information for considering my application, and understand that:

- *it will be treated confidentially at all times;*
- *if I am successful it will form part of my personnel records;*
- *if I am unsuccessful the information will be destroyed after six months.*

Signed: *Date:*

㉕ Stuart is a fundraising consultant. Some of his big clients carry out 'profiling' of potential wealthy donors. They collect a lot of information about the people's interests, friends and activities in order to build up a picture of the sort of support they are likely to give, before approaching them. Sometimes this takes several years. Stuart's main worry is that while this database is being compiled, the people do not know what is going on. Yet to tell them would destroy the whole purpose of the exercise.

Because most of the information going into the database is from the public domain, Stuart decides, with some hesitation, to rely on the 'disproportionate effort' argument and not to tell the people he is profiling. However, he realises that further clarification may be needed. In the meantime, reluctantly, he decides to leave out of the database anything which might be 'sensitive' data or which could not reasonably be said to be in the public domain.

㉖ Manesh needs to carry out extensive equal-opportunities monitoring of a youth training project. His manager suggests that the information collected could also be used to identify potential participants in special projects aimed at particular groups.

Manesh advises the manager that if they do this they cannot rely on the provisions for equalities monitoring, since they may end up using the information to make decisions about individuals. They therefore come up with the following statement for the form.

You do not have to provide any of this information, but if you do it will help us to make sure that you are getting the best help we can give you. We will not pass the information about you to anyone outside the Project, but we will compile statistics to show our funders and other people how we are doing. This form will be kept separate from our other information about you and your progress, and will be destroyed once you leave the Project.

Please sign here to show that you agree to us using the information on this form in the way we have described:

9
Data Subject rights

The 1998 Act introduces important new rights for Data Subjects, as well as strengthening and retaining rights which existed under the 1984 Act. For the first time individuals can actually prevent Data Controllers using their data in certain ways, either by withholding consent or by exercising specific rights. Some of these rights have been discussed above; the remainder are introduced in this chapter.

In summary, the Data Subjects' rights include the rights to:

- have specific information (see Chapter 8);
- consent, or not, to the use made of their data (see Chapter 6);
- opt out of direct marketing and tele-marketing (see Chapter 7);
- restrict automated decision-making (see below);
- prevent processing that causes harm to the Data Subject (see below);
- apply for Subject Access (see Chapter 10);
- ask the Data Protection Commissioner to make an 'Assessment' of whether an organisation or person is complying with the Act (see Chapter 14).

Automated decision-making

There are new rights in relation to automated decision-making processes, such as:

- credit scoring – if information is fed in and the decision on whether to grant someone credit is made entirely automatically;
- CV assessment – where a CV that is received electronically might be scanned automatically and rejected if the person is 'too old';
- automatically matching people as they pass in front of a CCTV camera against a file of photographs, to identify people who have been barred from the premises.

Since very few voluntary organisations have systems that make completely automatic decisions, these rights are described here in brief. Voluntary organisations might be able to help their clients to make use of these rights, and so do need to be aware of them.

As a Data Subject you have the right to 'require' a Data Controller, in writing, not to make any decisions about you entirely automatically.

If you have not done this, decisions may be made automatically, but you have the right to know 'as soon as reasonably practicable' that this is happening. You then have the right to ask for the decision to be reconsidered manually within 21 days. You can go to Court to enforce these rights if the Data Controller does not comply with them.

In brief, these rules do not apply if:

- the automatic decision is taken in connection with a legal responsibility or a contract involving you; *and*
- the effect of the decision is to grant your request *or* your interests are safeguarded (for example by allowing you to 'make representations').

What this means is that if, for example, you are turned down for credit, or a job, and the decision is made completely automatically, you must be told this and have the right for the decision to be reconsidered. But if you are given the credit you want, you don't have to be told. And if the final decision on whether to shortlist you for the job is checked by a person, you also have no rights to be told or to object.

Processing that harms the Data Subject

The Data Subject has the right to 'require' the Data Controller, in writing, to stop processing their personal data in ways that harm the Data Subject. Harm is defined as 'substantial damage or substantial distress' that is 'unwarranted'.

This right is available only if the Data Controller is relying on the fifth or sixth fair-processing conditions in Schedule 2: the official functions and the 'legitimate interests' of the Data Controller (see Conditions for fair processing on page 20). If the processing is in connection with a contract, for example, the Data Subject cannot prevent it.

If the right to stop processing is exercised, the Data Controller must reply in writing within 21 days, either agreeing to stop or saying why they don't think they should. The Data Subject can take the Data Controller to Court if they don't think they have complied properly.

Legal remedies

Many Data Protection problems will be resolved directly with the Data Controller or through the intervention of the Data Protection Commissioner. For most Data Subjects Court action will be a last resort. This section is therefore a very brief summary.

A Data Subject may use the Court to enforce other rights within the Act, such as those described immediately above and the right of Subject Access (see Chapter 10).

Where someone has suffered 'damage' by a contravention of the Act they can take the Data Controller to Court for compensation (and may also claim for associated distress).

The Court may order the Data Controller to 'rectify, block, erase or destroy' inaccurate data. This applies even if the mistake was made by someone else who provided the data. Alternatively the Court may order the Data Controller to add a statement to the record rebutting the inaccuracy. In addition the Court may order the Data Controller to notify anyone they have disclosed the inaccurate information to, if this is 'reasonably practicable'.

10

Subject Access

In principle a Data Subject has the right to know *all* the personal data that you hold about them. This is known as the right of Subject Access.

This right existed under the 1984 Act, but historically it has not been much used. Very few voluntary organisations have had experience of handling a Subject Access request. Nevertheless it is an important right, and if you are a Data Controller you need to be fully aware of it. The fact that under the 1998 Act it applies to manual data as well as computer records may well increase the number of Subject Access requests that are made.

The basic position is that when someone makes a valid Subject Access request you have to:

- tell them whether any of their personal data is being processed by you, or for you by a Data Processor;
- give them a description of the data, why you hold it and who it may be disclosed to;
- supply a copy of all the actual personal data you hold about that Data Subject;
- say where you got the information from, if you know;
- explain the 'logic' involved in any automated decision you make about that Data Subject, unless it is a trade secret.

There are qualifications to some of these provisions, discussed below.

What is a valid Subject Access request?

A Subject Access request must be made in writing; it may be sent by electronic means such as fax or e-mail.

You may, but do not have to, charge a fee of up to £10. There is nothing to stop you having a different fee for different circumstances, or different types of Data Subject. A Subject Access request is not valid until you have received any fee due.

You must be careful to provide the information only to the right person. This means that you may, and probably should, ask for information to verify their identity. You may also ask for information to help you locate their records. You might, for example, want to ask if they had ever been a client, or a volunteer, or which branch of your organisation they originally dealt with. A Subject Access request is not valid until you have received any of this information you need, but you can only ask for 'reasonable' information.

Once you have received a valid Subject Access request you must reply 'promptly' and within a maximum of 40 days.

You may choose to respond to an invalid Subject Access request (for example, one made verbally) if you wish.

You do not have to respond if a Subject Access request is made too soon after an identical or similar request from the same Data Subject. In deciding whether it is too soon, you have to consider the type of data, your purpose(s) in holding it, and how often it changes.

A Subject Access request form

You cannot insist on people using a specific form for making a Subject Access request, but you may feel that having one would help your Data Subjects. If you do, you could consider including sections that ask for:

- the name of the Data Subject (and any previous names);
- an address to which the reply should be sent;
- any information that you need to verify their identity;
- any information that you need to help you find the records;
- your fee;
- a signature. (Remember that normally one person can only act on behalf of another if they have the legal power to do so.)

It may be worth describing on the form the process that you will follow, and stating the time limit or any self-imposed targets for response. You may also want to give general information, for example about the purposes you process personal data for. A sample form is given overleaf.

What information do you have to provide?

In responding to a Subject Access request, you must in principle provide all the personal data you hold about the Data Subject. You must provide a copy of the information in 'permanent form', unless:

- it is not possible; or
- it would involve disproportionate effort; or
- the Data Subject has agreed otherwise.

Sample Subject Access request form

NAME OF ORGANISATION

Subject Access request (1998 Data Protection Act)

You are entitled to see most of the information we hold about you. If you want to see it, please fill in this form and hand it in to the office, with the £3 fee.

Your name:_____

Your address:_____

_____

_____

_____

A phone number where we can contact you (if you wish):_____

Please tick if you have ever been:

- ☐ a volunteer in our office
- ☐ a client at our main office
- ☐ a client at our branch office

If you have not ticked any of the above, please tell us of any reason why you think we might have information about you:_____

_____

If we may have known you under a different name, please tell us here:

_____

_____

If we find any information about you, do you want to:

- ☐ have a look at it at our office
- ☐ have us send you a copy

I want to see the records you hold on me, and I enclose £3.

Signature:_____

Please note:

- If the address you give above does not match the one in our records, we may have to ask you for additional identification.
- We will reply as quickly as we can. We aim to reply within three weeks, but we may take up to 40 days. If you have asked for a copy of the information, we will send it to the address you have given above.
- We have information about members of our organisation, staff, volunteers, clients, and people we think might be interested in our work. We don't keep this information once we no longer need it, so if you were in touch with us some time ago we may no longer have any information about you.
- We will show you everything we have about you, except that we may be allowed to hold back information which is also about someone else.

You must provide the information that you held at the time when the Subject Access request was made, except that you are allowed to make routine changes. For example, if you sell publications, and a customer asks for a copy of their record and, in the meantime, you receive a payment from them, you are allowed to update their record. You can even delete the information altogether *if you would have done it anyway*. For example, you might take people's details in order to send them a brochure, then delete the information once the brochure has been sent. Someone might make a Subject Access request only to find that by the time you responded you legitimately no longer held any information about them at all.

What you certainly must not do is tamper with the information to remove parts you would rather the Data Subject didn't see, or do anything to it that you wouldn't have done in the normal course of events.

Information you do not have to provide

When you respond to a Subject Access request you do not always have to include information that identifies an individual other than the Data Subject. You do have to include the information about the other person if:

- they have given their consent; or
- it is reasonable to go ahead without their consent.

In deciding whether it is reasonable to go ahead without consent, you have to take account of:

- any duty of confidentiality you owe to the other person;
- anything you have done to try to get their consent;
- whether they are able to give consent;
- whether they have refused consent.

These rules apply:

- either if the other person can be identified as the source of the information, or if they are just included in it – as a family member, a witness to an incident, even just a face in the background of a photograph; *and*
- if you have any reason to believe that the Data Subject could identify the other person. For example, in a dispute between neighbours, even an anonymous complaint might come from someone that the Data Subject can easily identify.

If you have consent, or if it is reasonable to go ahead without consent, then you *must* include the information about the other person in your response to the Subject Access request. You can also choose to include the information even if you don't have to, but you would have to be careful. For example, if the other person was also a Data Subject of yours, you would have to be sure that revealing the information when you didn't have to was 'fair'.

If you are certain that the information is something the Data Subject already knows – such as just the names of family members living in their house – you may be quite happy to release it without seeking consent. In other cases you may well want to check first whether you have any information about them that they would rather the Data Subject didn't see.

Where you regularly obtain information from other people, or where your records are likely to contain information about more than just the Data Subject, you may need to think ahead about whether you want to withhold it or not.

One option is to have an 'open files' policy. If people who give you information know in advance that it will be automatically shown to the Data Subject in response to a request, and that they will be identified, you would have good grounds for arguing that it was reasonable to give the information without going back to seek consent. This might be appropriate where the information comes from people who are providing it professionally (such as managers in a personnel system, or care workers in a client records system). They would have little reason to insist on anonymity.

In other cases you may want to assure people that the information they give will be held confidentially. Then you would have good grounds for withholding it from Subject Access.

Social work, medical and education exemptions

Parts of social work, medical and education records may be withheld from Subject Access in certain cases which are set out in supplementary Regulations.[21] The Act and Regulations define in detail which records are covered. Normally, records held by voluntary organisations are unlikely to be included. For example the social work exemptions apply to voluntary organisations only if:

- the organisation has been 'designated' by the Secretary of State for Health, *and*
- they are essentially carrying out local-authority social work functions.

The general ground for withholding information under all these Regulations is that disclosure would 'cause serious harm to the physical or mental health or condition of the Data Subject or another person'. In the case of medical records this has to be assessed by an appropriate medical practitioner. An employer could not, for example, decide for themselves to withhold the results of medical tests carried out on their behalf.

Practical steps

Although you may never have to deal with a Subject Access request, you do need to be prepared. Among other things, you should consider the following steps.

- All your staff and volunteers, particularly those who deal with clients or the public, must be made aware that a Subject Access request has a legal status

---

[21] Statutory Instruments 2000 Nos. 413, 414 and 415.

and that they must promptly pass it on to the appropriate person in the organisation.

- You may want to draw up a Subject Access request form.
- You should ensure when you design information systems that you make it as easy as possible to locate all the information about any particular Data Subject.
- Because you have to tell the Data Subject what sort of disclosures you make, and any information you have about the sources of your information, you may want to design systems to record your sources and disclosures.
- You may want to consider your policy on withholding information about other people (see above).
- Your Trustees or Management Committee will need to decide your policy on charging for Subject Access.

Summary

Individuals have a right to see most of the data you hold about them. You have to reply promptly to a Subject Access request, and within 40 days at most. You may charge up to £10 to reply to a Subject Access request.

You must generally provide, in permanent form, a copy of all the data about the Subject that you held at the time when the Subject Access request was made. In certain cases you are allowed to withhold access to information that identifies other people.

EXAMPLES

㉗ Lee is responsible for personnel administration in a medium-sized charity. One of the workers asks to see her file, but Lee is worried because the file contains an old note from her previous line manager that is not wholly complimentary. Suppressing the urge just to 'lose' the note, Lee has to decide whether there are any grounds for withholding it. He eventually concludes that he should not hold it back, since it was not given in confidence, and the line manager wrote it in the course of his work. For the future Lee resolves that personnel files should not contain this type of material in any case.

㉘ A mediation service does not always manage to win the trust of potential clients. Some of them start to make Subject Access requests in order to 'see what people are saying about me'. Linda, the manager, decides on a twofold strategy. Firstly, most of the records will be kept in paper files. Clients who have agreed to work with the service each get their own file, but until then the information is not readily accessible, and therefore not personal data. Secondly, the service will extend its policy on confidentiality, to make it clear that information provided by or related to other people will never be disclosed without their consent.

11

Security

The seventh Data Protection Principle says that a Data Controller must have appropriate security. There are two types of security breach you have to protect against:

- anyone seeing or using information that they shouldn't;
- data getting damaged, lost or destroyed.

The measures you take must be both technical (locks, passwords, back-ups and so on) and organisational (including training, supervision and management systems).

When a Data Controller has to make a notification (see Chapter 13), this must include a statement about the security measures in place. The Data Protection Commissioner has said that if a Data Controller has implemented BS7799 (the British Standard for Information Security Management) this will represent the type of assurance that the Commissioner is looking for. The questions asked on the notification application form reflect the approach taken by BS7799, and you are prompted to confirm that you broadly follow that approach.

BS7799 itself is complex and expensive to implement, and is unlikely to be worth pursuing for most voluntary organisations. This does not mean that security can be ignored, however.

What is 'appropriate'?

The security measures you need to take will depend very much on the sensitivity (in its ordinary sense) of the data you process. Your approach should be similar to that in a risk assessment.

- How many people could be harmed by any specific risk?
- How likely is it to happen?
- How great would the damage be if it did?

Information which you could easily replace would obviously not merit such great security as that which would take considerable time and effort to replace, or which may be completely irreplaceable. Highly confidential information would need more protection than that which is already in the public domain.

Some of your security measures will be general, and aimed at protecting you against disruption as much as anything. Making back-ups and checking incoming electronic material for viruses should be part of everyone's routine procedures. So should making sure that you know who is in the building, and that strangers are not allowed to wander around unsupervised.

You should also take those specific additional measures which protect most effectively against the most serious risks. With confidential client files, for example, you may want to have a procedure for signing them in and out of a secure area, to allow for times when your staff may need to take material out to meetings or case conferences. If you regularly deliver some of your services off the premises – at outreach sessions or in people's homes, for example – this might be a particular concern.

If staff or volunteers work from home at all you will need to think about how to ensure that your security measures extend to their laptops (which may get stolen), their home computers (which may be used by other family members), or their kitchen tables, which are all intrinsically insecure areas.

Access control

In order to prevent people gaining unauthorised access to information, you may need to consider any or all of the following questions.

- Do your staff members and volunteers know which information they are allowed to see and which not?
- Have your staff and volunteers been trained or briefed on how to keep data secure?
- Are your confidential files in a protected area and/or locked away when not in use?
- Are you careful not to allow unauthorised people to be left on their own in the presence of personal data?
- Do you clear your working area of personal data before leaving the office (and letting the cleaners in)?
- Are your computers sited so that people cannot see material on the screen that they shouldn't?
- Do you encrypt or password-protect personal data, especially when you send it by e-mail?
- Is your Web site isolated from your internal systems and protected from hackers?

- Do you have a system to keep track of personal data that people take out of the office?
- Does your system prevent people from leaving personal data on the screen for too long (for example when they leave their desk, or when the next client has already arrived)?
- If people are allowed to see some material, but not all of it, do your systems help to enforce this, by storing the information in different places or by requiring a different password for the more sensitive material?
- When you deliberately delete material from your computer, do you have the facility to overwrite it to make sure that it is irrecoverable?
- Do you force people to change passwords and access codes often enough (especially when staff leave)?
- Do you require external contractors (such as computer maintenance staff) to give confidentiality undertakings?
- Are confidential manual files shredded or securely disposed of?

Loss or damage

Data in electronic form is particularly vulnerable to loss or damage as a result of computer failure and other technical problems. Manual data must not be overlooked, however. You may need to consider the following questions.

- Are your staff and volunteers aware of all the precautions they need to take? Have they been trained in back-up and other procedures?
- Are irreplaceable documents protected from fire (especially if you ever hold original documents on behalf of service users)?
- Do you avoid taking irreplaceable documents out of the building whenever possible?
- Are your computer systems rigorously and frequently enough backed up, using a recognised procedure?
- Do you test your back-ups to ensure they can be restored?
- Do your computer users know how to set their software to make automatic back-ups?
- Do you protect your organisation against computer viruses?
- Do your systems require confirmation before significant material can be deleted?
- Do you give meaningful and consistent names to your files, so that they are less likely to be deleted inadvertently?
- Have you taken adequate precautions to avoid key computers being stolen?
- Do your staff and volunteers take steps to protect computers against damage, especially from liquids or physical damage?
- Do you have a disaster-recovery plan?

British Standard 7799

BS7799 identifies 10 key 'controls' for information security.

- Is there a documented security policy?
- Are responsibilities for security processes clearly allocated?
- Are users given adequate security training?
- Are security incidents always reported?
- Is there a virus-checking policy?
- Is there a plan for maintaining business continuity?
- Are legal copyright issues always given due consideration?
- Are important organisational records protected?
- Are personal records processed in accordance with the Data Protection Act?
- Are regular security reviews performed?

These controls provide for the basic level of information security. However, BS7799 also covers measures necessary to achieve a higher level of security, including:

- more on policies and management of security;
- asset classification and control;
- personnel security;
- physical and environmental security;
- computer and network management;
- system access control;
- systems development and maintenance;
- business continuity planning;
- compliance with all relevant laws.

These headings are worth consideration by any organisation which is drawing up its own security policy.

Implementing BS7799 itself is carried out on a commercial basis by the British Standards Institution and other bodies. It involves assessment, advice and audit procedures, and leads to certification which lasts for three years.

Summary

- You must have security measures that are appropriate to the type of personal data you hold and to how it is used. These must prevent unauthorised access as well as inadvertent loss or damage.
- You must describe your security measures when you notify your processing to the Data Protection Commissioner.
- BS7799 covers Information Security Management, but is complex and expensive to implement.

EXAMPLES

㉙ Malcolm runs a dial-a-ride service. One day, one of the drivers leaves his pick-up list on top of the minibus by mistake and drives off. The details of his clients, including when they will be away from home and information about their disabilities, go floating off for anyone to find.

Malcolm realises that this is a potentially serious security breach. He modifies the minibus dashboard so that there is a recognised place to secure the pick-up lists. He changes procedures so that the lists have to be signed in and out, and briefs all the staff on why he has done this. He reports to the committee, which is satisfied that he has taken 'appropriate' technical and organisational measures both to improve security and to ensure that any future problem is identified as early as possible.

㉚ Most of the volunteers at Sarah's drop-in centre for elderly people come from the local community. One day she overhears two of them exchanging gossip about several of the centre users, which they have picked up in the course of their work. Some of the information is 'sensitive'. Sarah quickly stops them, and realises that many of the volunteers are likely to know users of the centre, or have them as neighbours. In this situation it is particularly important to be responsible about the use of information they acquire about users. Sarah organises a training session for all the volunteers on confidentiality, and strengthens the centre's policy so that volunteers have to sign a statement clearly agreeing not to discuss with each other any information which is in the client files.

㉛ Martha works at a large residential home. A new computer system is introduced for holding residents' details, which includes a lot of 'sensitive' information. The centre manager and shift leaders are trained in how to use it, and given passwords which allow access to all the information, while other workers are allowed to access only basic parts of the record.

One day Martha needs to look up the phone number of a resident's daughter to discuss a change of room with her. When she goes to the computer she finds that the centre manager has been using it, and has been called away urgently, leaving the database open on a very sensitive screen which Martha is normally not able to see. Martha hasn't been told what to do in this situation, or how to close the screen and get back to her normal view of the data. She mentions the incident to her shift leader.

The shift leader's first response is to blame Martha for getting unauthorised access to the data, but Martha manages to convince him that it wasn't her fault. Instead, they compile a report to the information steering group. The group concludes that:

- the centre manager should not have left the screen open; however, since she was called away in a genuine emergency, they decide to take no further action;
- it would be better if the system was redesigned to shut down sensitive screens automatically after a set interval of no activity;
- all staff should be given extra training in what to do if they find the system behaving differently from usual.

12

Transferring personal data abroad

The eighth Data Protection Principle imposes restrictions on the transfer of information outside the European Economic Area (the countries of the European Union[22] plus Norway, Iceland and Liechtenstein). The Principle is modified by Schedule 4 of the Act.

The aim of the Principle is to ensure that Data Subjects do not lose any of their rights when their personal data is transferred abroad. The Principle therefore states that data can only be transferred abroad if the destination country has adequate Data Protection provision. Very few countries have legislation equivalent to that of the UK,[23] which makes the question of assessing adequacy fairly complicated. Most of the discussion around this part of the Act has concentrated on the United States of America, which has made it clear that it does not regard Data Protection as a suitable subject for national legislation, preferring to see it as a contractual matter between the Data Subject and the Data Controller.

The Data Protection Commissioner has issued preliminary guidance on how to assess the adequacy of contractual or other measures for protecting the Data Subject's rights, which would allow transfer abroad to take place. At the time of writing, negotiations were still underway in a number of areas, so the situation may well change.

The Data Protection Commissioner states that:

'Data Controllers are required to make a judgement as to whether the level of protection afforded by all the circumstances of the case is commensurate with the potential risks to the rights and freedoms of Data Subjects in relation to the processing of personal data.'[24]

---

[22] Currently these are Austria, Belgium, Denmark, Finland, France, Germany, Greece, Ireland, Italy, Luxembourg, the Netherlands, Portugal, Spain, Sweden and the United Kingdom.

[23] It is understood at the time of writing that only Hong Kong and New Zealand are considered by the Data Protection Commissioner to have acceptable legislation.

[24] *The Eighth Data Protection Principle and Transborder Dataflows: the Data Protection Registrar's legal analysis and suggested 'good practice approach' to assessing adequacy including consideration of the issue of contractual solutions*. Undated. Obtained from the Data Protection Web site on 2 December 1999.

The guidance then goes into considerable detail on a 'good practice' approach to transferring data abroad. Rather than duplicate what is, after all, only provisional guidance, it is recommended that you contact the Data Protection Commissioner for the most up-to-date guidance if any of your processing involves transferring personal data abroad.

Schedule 4 permits the eighth Principle to be overridden if, among other things:

- the Data Subject has given consent; *or*
- the data has to be transferred in connection with a contract involving the Data Subject; *or*
- the terms of the transfer are approved or authorised by the Data Protection Commissioner.

The main problem with deriving 'terms' that the Commissioner can approve appears to have been that until recently the law in England and Wales (unlike in Scotland) did not permit a contract between two parties to grant rights to a third party. This meant that a Data Controller in England or Wales could not gain contractual rights for a Data Subject by means of a contract with a recipient organisation abroad. However, the law has recently been amended in this regard.[25] Wherever possible the Commissioner will support the development of model contractual clauses which may be used to protect Data Subject rights when data is transferred abroad.

Personal data on the Web

Those voluntary organisations that routinely transfer personal data to organisations abroad will obviously need to go further into the question of how to comply with the eighth Data Protection Principle. But if you put information onto the Web you also need to be aware that you are, in effect, transferring it abroad, and therefore subject to the Principle.

Since the data is, by definition, going outside the European Economic Area, and the recipients are unknown, contractual or other protections are unlikely to be available. In some cases you may decide that the data is so trivial that a total lack of protection is, nevertheless, 'adequate'. In many other cases, however, this will not be the case. For these, it will almost always be necessary to seek the consent of the Data Subject in order to avoid the need to comply with the Principle. For this purpose, ordinary, rather than 'explicit', consent would be required (see Chapter 6).

Summary

Transferring information abroad from the UK is within the Act if one or more of these conditions is met:

- it is going within the European Economic Area;
- the country it is going to has adequate Data Protection provision;

---

[25] The Contracts (Rights of Third parties) Act 1999, which applies to all contracts entered into after 11 May 2000.

- you have the consent of the Data Subject;
- it is in connection with a contract involving the Data Subject;
- the interests of the Data Subject are protected by an approved contract;
- the Data Protection Commissioner has authorised it;
- it complies with a limited number of other circumstances.

Putting personal data on the Web almost certainly needs consent from the Data Subject.

13
Notification

One of the fundamental differences between the new Act and the old one concerns registration, now renamed notification. Under the 1984 Act, the very first question was 'Do we need to register?' If you did, the Act applied to you. If you didn't have to register, that was the end of the story and the Act did not apply.

All that has changed. The first question now is 'Are we a Data Controller?' If you are, all the preceding chapters of this book apply, and your responsibilities under the 1998 Act are considerable. A Data Controller may, in addition, have to 'notify' the Data Protection Commissioner; on the other hand they may not, as there are many exemptions from notification. The key point is that the Data Protection Principles and other provisions of the Act apply regardless. The question of notification is no longer central to everyone who is processing personal data.

However, for those who do have to notify, it does matter. Failing to notify when you should is a 'strict liability' criminal offence: you have no excuse if you get it wrong. 'I did my best' is not enough.

Do you need to notify?

You don't need to notify at all if all your processing of personal data is exempt. The Data Protection Commissioner publishes a useful free booklet, *Notification exemptions: a self-assessment guide.*

The exemptions fall into two main categories.

- Manually held data is completely exempt from notification, under the terms of the Act itself. If you notify a system that is partly held manually and partly on computer, you have to indicate just that there is additional manual material.
- Certain 'core business purposes' have been exempted from notification by Regulation,[26] even if the data is held on computer.

The core business purposes are:

- personnel administration, including payroll, and including volunteers;
- accounts and customer/supplier records;

---

[26] Statutory Instrument 2000 No. 188.

- marketing, promotion and public relations (which might well, for example, cover a mailing list used to send out annual reports and other general promotional material);
- membership records of non-profit organisations.

In each case there are limitations. Generally the Data Subjects, the types of data held, and any disclosures must be restricted to those 'necessary' for the purpose, in order to claim the exemption.

You may voluntarily notify activities that are exempt. The advantage of this is that by notification you 'specify' the purposes for which you are obtaining data. If you don't notify you have to specify the purposes directly to each of your Data Subjects.

Who has to notify?

Notification must be made by the Data Controller. Remember that you cannot be a Data Controller on someone else's behalf. Therefore, each Data Controller has to consider separately whether notification is required. A charity may be exempt while its associated trading company has to notify. A national organisation may need to notify while some of its local branches are exempt but others, perhaps because they keep information on computer rather than manually, also have to notify.

Notification procedure

Notification can be initiated in two ways:

- by phone, to the Data Protection Commissioner – at the time of writing the number is 01625 545740;
- on the Internet – at the time of writing the Web address is www.dpr.gov.uk

In either case you will first have to provide details of the Data Controller. Guidance is available from the Data Protection Commissioner on how to complete these details. For example, in the case of a limited company you have to provide the full company name, not a trading name. An individual has to provide their full name.

In an attempt to simplify the notification process, once you have indicated the general nature of your activities the Data Protection Commissioner will generate a draft notification based on 'typical' activities for that type of business. This will be sent to you (if you phoned up), or can be printed off (if you used the Internet). You make any corrections necessary, sign it, and send it off with the fee.

The bulk of the notification is concerned with the Purposes for which you process data. You are offered a list of standard Purposes to choose from (see box below). For each Purpose that applies to you, you then have to specify your Data Subjects, Data Classes, potential recipients of data and any overseas transfers of personal data.

If the draft you receive from the Data Protection Commissioner does not accurately reflect what you do, you can add or delete Purposes and, within each Purpose, Data Subjects, Data Classes, recipients and overseas transfers. In each case you can make up your own entry if the standard ones really don't apply. You cannot normally use a Purpose twice.

One feature from the 1984 registration scheme which is missing from notification is the need to indicate your sources of information. In addition the standard lists of potential Data Subjects, Data Classes and recipients are significantly shorter. It should therefore be easier to decide whether or not they apply, making completion of the forms both quicker and more accurate.

In the final part of the notification you have to describe in general terms your security measures (see Chapter 11 for more on this), together with various other pieces of additional information.

Notification costs £35 per year for each Data Controller, regardless of how many purposes you have. This means that if any of your purposes at all have to be notified it costs nothing for you voluntarily to add any other purposes for which you process personal data, even if they are exempt. No Data Controller can have more than one notification.

If you have decided that you and one or more other organisations are joint Data Controllers for a particular activity, it may well be worth coordinating your notification efforts to ensure consistency.

It may be attractive for national organisations to produce model notification entries, as guidance for local groups. If they do this, it must be made clear that any local group cannot just use the model without checking that it really does reflect their activities.

After notification

Once your notification has been accepted it remains valid for one year. Near the end of that time the Data Protection Commissioner will remind you to renew it.

You have to keep your notification up to date. So if any of the details change, either about the Data Controller or about your activities, you have to ensure that an amendment form is submitted within 28 days. There is no charge for this. Failure to do it is a criminal offence.

You cannot transfer your notification. This means that if you change your legal status (for example, by becoming a limited company or amalgamating with another organisation) the new organisation has to notify from scratch in its own right.

Standard purposes, data subjects and data classes for notification

Standard purposes

Staff administration

Advertising, marketing and public relations

Accounts and records

Accounting and auditing (for other people)

Administration of justice

Administration of membership records

Advertising, marketing and public relations for others

Assessment and collection of taxes and other revenue

Benefits, grants and loans administration

Canvassing political support amongst the electorate

Constituency casework

Consultancy and advisory services

Credit referencing

Crime prevention and prosecution of offenders

Debt administration and factoring

Education

Fundraising

Health administration and services

Information and databank administration

Insurance administration

Journalism and media

Legal services

Licensing and registration

Pastoral care

Pensions administration

Policing

Private investigation

Processing for not-for-profit organisations (membership & related services)

Property management

Provision of financial services and advice

Realising the objectives of a charitable organisation or voluntary body

Research

Trading/sharing in personal information

In nearly all cases the Data Protection Commissioner goes on to expand on what each of these purposes is expected to cover.

Data Subjects

S100 Staff, including volunteers, agents, temporary and casual workers
S101 Customers and clients
S102 Suppliers
S103 Members or supporters
S104 Complainants, correspondents and enquirers
S105 Relatives, guardians and associates of the Data Subject
S106 Advisers, consultants and other professional experts
S107 Patients
S108 Students and pupils
S109 Offenders and suspected offenders

Data classes

C200 Personal details
C201 Family, lifestyle and social circumstances
C202 Education and training details
C203 Employment details
C204 Financial details
C205 Goods or services provided
C206 Racial or ethnic origin
C207 Political opinions
C208 Religious or other beliefs of a similar nature
C209 Trade union membership
C210 Physical or mental health or condition
C211 Sexual life
C212 Offences (including alleged offences)
C213 Criminal proceedings, outcomes and sentences

Summary

- Any data controller may, potentially, have to notify the Data Protection Commissioner about their Data Protection activities.
- Notification can be initiated only by telephone or on the notification Web site, where further guidance is available.
- The annual fee is £35, regardless of the size or complexity of the activities being notified.
- Certain activities (including all manual processing) are exempt from notification. However, this does not exempt them from any other aspect of the Act.
- Exempt activities may be notified voluntarily.
- Failure to notify when it is required is an offence.

⌇14
Enforcement

The Data Protection Act is enforced by the Data Protection Commissioner, currently Elizabeth France. The Commissioner also enforces the Telecommunications (Data Protection and Privacy) Regulations 1999. The Commissioner's Office is an independent regulatory authority, reporting directly to Parliament.

The Commissioner does not have a large staff – around 100 – and is funded by income from notification fees and other charges, not by government grant.

The 1998 Act has considerably strengthened the enforcement powers of the Commissioner, and her staff for the first time have powers of entry and inspection when they are investigating breaches of the Act.

Codes of practice

An important new provision in the 1998 Act is that the Data Protection Commissioner now has both a power and a duty to promote good practice. In particular she can endorse Codes of Practice for particular types of activity or industry sectors. If she believes a Code of Practice is necessary and the industry has not produced one, she can even impose one of her own.

At the time of writing, no Codes of Practice with particular relevance to the voluntary sector have been produced. These would, however, be a welcome development, and it is very likely that national federations and other interest groups will produce relevant Codes of Practice in future.

Notification

Notification is one aspect of enforcement. Processing without having notified when you should have done so is an offence. This is a 'strict liability' offence: you cannot argue that you did your best. It is also an offence not to keep your notification up to date. On this you *can* argue that you exercised 'due diligence'.

Assessments

Anyone may ask the Data Protection Commissioner to make an Assessment as to whether a Data Controller appears to be complying with the Act. The person making the request must believe themselves to be directly affected by the processing they want assessed. The Commissioner *must* then make an Assessment, provided she has enough information to identify the person making the request and the processing in question.

The Commissioner can choose how to make the Assessment. She can specifically take into account:

- whether the request raises a matter of substance;
- any undue delay in making the request;
- whether the person is entitled to make a Subject Access request.

What this appears to mean is that requests for Assessment should not be used when the matter could have been resolved directly with the Data Controller or through a Subject Access request. If the Commissioner thinks this is the case, it may affect how the Assessment is carried out.

The Commissioner has to tell the person making the request whether she has made an Assessment, and may – but is not obliged to – tell them the outcome.

An Assessment is only the Commissioner's opinion, but would obviously carry some weight if the matter later came to Court.

Information notices

The Commissioner may issue a Data Controller with an Information Notice, either as part of an Assessment or for reasons of her own. This will ask the Data Controller to provide specific information within a specified time limit, with the aim of enabling the Commissioner to decide whether the Data Protection Principles are being complied with.

Failure to comply with an Information Notice is an offence, unless the Data Controller can show that they 'exercised due diligence' to comply. The Data Controller can appeal against an Information Notice to the Data Protection Tribunal.

Enforcement notices

Where the Commissioner is satisfied that the Act has been contravened she can issue an Enforcement Notice, telling the Data Controller what they must do in order to bring their activities into line.

Failure to comply with an Enforcement Notice is an offence, unless the Data Controller can show that they 'exercised due diligence' to comply. The Data

Controller can appeal against an Enforcement Notice to the Data Protection Tribunal.

Powers of entry

The Commissioner can apply for a warrant from a circuit judge to enter and inspect premises if she has reasonable grounds for suspecting that an offence under the Act has been committed or the Data Protection Principles are being broken.

The warrant may be granted only if the Data Protection Commissioner has tried to get access by agreement and been refused, unless the judge is convinced that giving advance warning would defeat the object.

It is a criminal offence to obstruct a warrant, with a maximum fine of £5,000.

Individual offences

In addition to the offence of obstructing a warrant, individuals commit an offence if they 'knowingly or recklessly' obtain or disclose personal data without consent from the Data Controller. Possible defences include having the 'reasonable belief' that what they did was permissible.

If a person has obtained data they are not entitled to, it is a further offence to sell it or offer to sell it.

It may be worth making staff and volunteers who have access to personal data aware of these provisions.

Penalties

All offences under the Act, except obstructing a warrant, can be tried either in the Magistrate's Court or the Crown Court. The maximum penalty is a fine of £5,000 in the Magistrate's Court or an unlimited fine in the Crown Court.

Who gets taken to Court, should it come to that, depends on the offence. Where the offence is an individual one, it is obviously the individual who would be charged. Where the organisation has committed an offence to do with notification or not cooperating with the Commissioner, the organisation would be charged. However, an unincorporated association (see Appendix A) *cannot* be taken to Court in its own right. In this case it would most likely be all the members of the Management Committee who would end up being personally charged.

If your organisation is incorporated, the directors or senior officers may also be *personally liable* if they consented to or connived at the offence, or if they were negligent.

Summary

The 1998 Data Protection Act is enforced by the Data Protection Commissioner.

The Commissioner can:

- make an Assessment;
- issue an Information Notice;
- issue an Enforcement Notice;
- apply for a warrant to enter and inspect premises.

Failure to notify and failure to keep a notification up to date are offences.

Individuals commit an offence if they knowingly or recklessly get access to data without permission, and a second offence if they then try to sell it.

The maximum penalty for any offence is £5,000 if tried in the Magistrate's Court, but most can also be tried in the Crown Court, with unlimited fines.

15
Exemptions

Very little, if any, personal data is totally exempt from the 1998 Act. In specific cases, however, some or all of the Data Protection Principles do not apply. In other cases the Data Subject does not have to be provided with information that they may otherwise be entitled to, or you may be allowed to make a disclosure which would not normally be permitted.

Domestic use

Personal data processed *by an individual* only for their 'personal, family or household affairs (including recreational purposes)' is exempt from:

- all the Data Protection Principles;
- Subject Access and other individual rights;
- notification.

This would clearly not apply to the use of a home computer on behalf of a group or organisation, and it would be important to establish whether the Data Controller was the group or the individual.

Even where the exemption applies, the Data Protection Commissioner still has enforcement powers; in other words she could still issue an Information Notice to check on what you were doing.

National security

There are wide-ranging exemptions that apply to national security, including exemption from all the Data Protection Principles.

'Subject information' exemptions

Some of the specific exemptions modify the rules on '**subject information**'. If such an exemption applies:

- you do not have to tell the Data Subject that you are processing their data (see Chapter 4);
- the Data Subject does not have the right of Subject Access.

As well as the specific restrictions on Subject Access to some social work, health and education records (see Chapter 10), these may also be exempt from the 'subject information provisions' in certain circumstances.

There are other exemptions to the 'subject information provisions' for areas such as negotiations, management planning and academic examinations. This means that, for example, you may not have to reveal details of your future plans to a staff member who makes a Subject Access request.

'Non-disclosure' exemptions

Other exemptions modify the normal restrictions on '**non-disclosure**'. If such an exemption applies you can make a *disclosure* of the data, even if it would conflict with some of the Data Protection Principles. The ones you are allowed to break in making the disclosure are:

- the part of the first Data Protection Principle which says that all processing must be fair (but you must still meet at least one of the conditions for fair processing and the conditions for sensitive data, if applicable);
- the Principles that say you must only use the data for the specified purpose, and that it has to be adequate, relevant, not excessive, accurate, up-to-date and not held longer than necessary.

Also under this exemption, the Data Subject cannot prevent disclosure under the provision for preventing processing likely to cause damage or distress (see Chapter 9), and cannot get inaccurate data changed (see Chapter 10).

For voluntary organisations the main impact is likely to be the exemption from the 'non-disclosure provisions' in *any case* where the disclosure is for one of the 'crime and taxation' purposes, which are:

- the prevention or detection of crime;
- the apprehension or prosecution of offenders; or
- the assessment or collection of any tax or duty.

The exemption can be invoked only if applying the normal rules would be 'likely to prejudice' the purpose. The Act does not say that you *must* disclose in these circumstances, merely that if you do, you have not breached the Data Protection Act.

A further exemption from non-disclosure restrictions applies where the law *requires* you to reveal information.

Other exemptions

There are various exemptions allowing data to be processed for research, history and statistics, even where this was not the original purpose for its collection.

These allow data held for these purposes to be kept indefinitely and to be used regardless of the purpose(s) they were originally obtained for, provided that:

- the processing does not support actions or decisions relating to specific individuals; *and*
- the processing does not cause anyone substantial damage or distress.

There is a 'freedom of expression' exemption from all the Data Protection Principles except the seventh Principle (Security) for genuine journalistic, artistic and literary purposes. The Act specifies the conditions which have to be met for this to apply. These include that the processing must be for publication and in the public interest.

If your organisation is involved in publishing or other relevant activities, further details of this exemption may be worth pursuing.

Summary

Apart from broad exemptions for domestic use and for national security, most of the exemptions from the Act are restricted to particular actions and under particular circumstances.

16
What to do next

Although the Act is complex, common sense and a broad understanding of the Data Protection Principles will in the main ensure that you don't go far wrong. You may want to consider the following suggestions.

- Draw up a policy on Data Protection (perhaps linked to your confidentiality policy).
- Train or brief your staff in what they are allowed to do with people's information, what they are not allowed to do, and who they have to ask if they are unsure.
- Ensure that anyone you hold information about knows that you hold it, what you use it for, and who you might pass it on to.
- Get consent for holding people's information wherever possible, and get explicit consent, in writing if possible, for any sensitive information you want to hold.
- Make sure that you offer people the chance to opt out of any direct marketing, including fundraising.
- Design or modify your systems so that you can easily comply with any Subject Access request, and make sure that you have suitable Subject Access arrangements.
- Make appropriate security arrangements, for both manual and computer systems, depending on how sensitive the information is.
- Ensure that you have an appropriate policy on archiving and destruction.
- Check whether you need to 'notify' the Data Protection Commissioner about your data-processing activities.
- Appoint a member of staff as Data Protection Compliance Officer, so that they know it is part of their job to find out about Data Protection in more detail and to keep the organisation within the law.

Data Protection policies

If you are drawing up a policy explaining your approach to Data Protection you are likely to want to focus particularly on the types of Data Subjects on whom you hold substantial amounts of information, or where it is especially confidential or sensitive. Your policy could cover:

- why you hold the information, including any secondary uses you make of it;
- what types of information you hold;
- whether you collect any information without the Data Subject knowing;
- the types of disclosure you are likely to make;
- how you ensure that the information is accurate;
- for how long you keep the information;
- what level of confidentiality you apply;
- any special security measures that apply.

Specific considerations

The following sections each flag up some of the areas that may be particularly relevant to the various systems and sets of information that you hold.

Personnel records

These may include systems holding data about permanent employees, volunteers, contract or casual staff and job applicants.

Key questions to ask include:

- If some of the data is sensitive (e.g. health information, criminal record), has the Data Subject given explicit consent to its use (e.g. on the application form)?
- If the data is to be used in any non-obvious way, has the Data Subject been informed?
- If the data is to be passed to other Data Controllers (including other related organisations) is the Data Subject told that this might happen?
- Where a 'secondary' Data Subject's details are captured (e.g. as next of kin), do they know? Has the Data Subject been asked to ensure that they know?
- What happens to unsuccessful applications? Is there a policy on how long they need to be kept, and are they then destroyed?
- What happens when employees or volunteers leave? Is the data reduced to the minimum necessary and then archived?
- Is there a policy on who is authorised to see personnel information?
- Are there appropriate security measures? Do these cover job application forms and other data-capture documents, and do they cover destruction procedures for confidential material?
- If anyone's details are put onto the Web, have they given consent?
- When references are sought, is it clear to the referee what access the employee will have to the file containing the reference?

Areas where action may need to be taken include:

- Application forms may have to be redesigned, to provide Data Subjects with the necessary information and to get consent for collecting sensitive data.
- Your contract may need clauses spelling out your employees' responsibility for following Data Protection procedures, and including statements you may need to make about your use of employee data.
- Volunteer agreements may also need to be amended.
- You must ensure that you can respond to Subject Access requests for personnel information.

Client records

These can include any information you collect about people who use your services, including people who pay for publications or training and people who enquire for information without becoming regular clients.

Key questions to ask include:

- Do the Data Subjects know who is collecting their details and why? (If the identity of the Data Controller is not obvious, or if data is obtained from another Data Controller, this should be stated.)
- If some of the data is sensitive (e.g. health information), has the Data Subject given explicit consent to its use (e.g. on a form confirming that they want you to provide services, and giving consent to act on their behalf, if appropriate)?
- If you collect sensitive personal data about clients over the phone, are you sure that you have reliable procedures in place to obtain and record consent?
- Do all your staff and volunteers know their Data Protection responsibilities?
- If the data is to be used in any non-obvious way, has the Data Subject been informed?
- If the data is to be passed to other Data Controllers (e.g. in the course of providing advice, support or other services) is the Data Subject told that this might happen?
- Is there a policy on how long data needs to be kept, and is it then destroyed?
- Is there a policy on who is authorised to see the data?
- Are there appropriate security measures, especially where material is taken away from secure areas in the office?
- Has this use been included in your Data Protection Notification?

Areas where action may need to be taken include:

- providing information about data protection and the option to consent on all your forms, leaflets and notices, and in interviews and on the telephone if appropriate;

- arranging for explicit consent procedures if required for sensitive data;
- guidance for all staff and volunteers in contact with clients;
- clarity on confidentiality and disclosures of information;
- policies on the archive and destruction of data;
- security procedures;
- provision for Subject Access;
- notification.

Professionals and contacts in other organisations

This would include any individuals whose details are kept, either because of their professional role (e.g. social workers), or as contacts within another organisation for any reason.

Key questions to ask include:

- Is the data being held for a specific purpose or purposes, and is it used only in a manner compatible with these purpose(s)?
- If the data is to be used in any non-obvious way, has the Data Subject been informed?
- If you are going to publish the personal data at all (e.g. in a directory) does the individual know, and do you have their consent (or are you *sure* you don't need it)?
- Is there a policy on how long data needs to be kept, and is it then destroyed?
- If the data is to be used for any kind of direct marketing to the individuals (as opposed to the organisation they represent), has the Data Subject been informed and been given the opportunity to opt out?
- If the Data Subject's details are put onto the Web, have they given consent?

Areas where action may need to be taken include:

- Data Protection statements in standard letters;
- guidance to staff on the purpose(s) for which data is collected, and limits on what it may be used for;
- provision for respecting opt-outs regarding direct marketing.

Records of members or donors

This would cover anyone you have on your database because they support your organisation, or might support it in future, as well as official 'members'.

Key questions to ask include:

- Do the Data Subjects know how their data will be used (e.g. for marketing by an associated trading company, for publication in a directory, in mailing-list exchanges with other organisations)?
- Do you have clear, well-publicised and straightforward procedures for people to opt out of direct marketing, including fundraising?

- Do you have clear policies on the circumstances in which you will, or won't, exchange membership data with other organisations or carry out reciprocal mailings?
- Do all your staff and volunteers know what they can and can't do with membership data?
- Do you have clear policies on how long to keep data about people who drop out or stop replying when you try to contact them?

Areas where action may need to be taken include:

- clear and unambiguous Data Protection statements/consents in literature to new members and, from time to time, existing ones;
- guidance to staff and volunteers;
- provision for opt-outs from direct marketing and fundraising;
- provision for opt-outs from disclosure or list-sharing (including to linked trading companies);
- database design to take account of your Data Protection responsibilities, including respecting all relevant opt-outs.

Research data

This would include any identifiable individuals whose details are acquired as part of research projects.

Key questions to ask include:

- Do the Data Subjects know who is using their details and why? (If the identity of the Data Controller is not obvious, or if the data has been passed on from another Data Controller, this information should be provided.)
- Is the data being held for a specific purpose or purposes, and is it used only in a manner compatible with these purpose(s)?
- If the data is to be used in any non-obvious way, has the Data Subject been informed? Do they know the form in which data may be disclosed, especially if this will not be anonymous?
- If the data is to be passed to other Data Controllers, is the Data Subject told that this might happen?
- Is there a policy on how long data needs to be kept, and is it then destroyed? If data is to be kept indefinitely, do the Data Subjects know this?
- Are there appropriate security measures?
- Has this use been included in your notification?

Areas where action may need to be taken include:

- Data Protection statements at the time when data is collected;
- guidance to staff and volunteers, including temporary research assistants, on the purpose(s) for which data is collected and limits on how it may be used;
- notification.

Collaborative arrangements

This would include any occasions when two Data Controllers within your own organisation collaborate, or when you work jointly with external organisations.

Key questions to ask include:

- Has it been established who the Data Controller is, or is the responsibility shared?
- Is the relationship spelled out in writing?
- Are both parties satisfied with their own and each other's security procedures?
- Is it clear for what purpose(s) personal data is being collected?
- Has provision been made for giving Data Subjects the information they require?
- Has provision been made for gaining and recording Data Subject consent where necessary?
- Has provision been made for handling Subject Access?
- Are there any Notification implications?

Areas where action may need to be taken include:

- written and contractual arrangements;
- agreement on procedures;
- provision for checking each other's security;
- notification.

Networks and federations

Although this book is aimed principally at front-line voluntary organisations, there is clearly a role for second-tier bodies in work concerning Data Protection. Where members of a network or federation are carrying out similar work they may well be able to benefit from each other's experience or to share the effort of producing documentation and procedures. The network or federation could get involved in:

- producing clear standards that members are expected to follow;
- drafting model statements, policies and procedures;
- identifying centres of excellence that other members can learn from;
- offering legal advice;
- advice on system design.

A network or federation may also wish to consider whether it would have a role in working with the Data Protection Commissioner to produce a Code of Practice for its area of work (see Chapter 14).

Database design

Anyone designing or modifying a database can do much to help you comply with the Data Protection Act by building in specific features. The following is not necessarily an exhaustive list, but may provide a good starting point.

- You must be able to retrieve and print out absolutely all the information about a particular individual easily and in a digestible form, in case they make a Subject Access request.
- You must build in appropriate security measures, including access controls and back-up procedures.
- You must be able to record which people have opted out of direct marketing, and then suppress their record as appropriate, for example when you print labels for a mailshot, or phone numbers for a telephone campaign.
- You should think about whether you need to record whether and how consent was given by the Data Subject for the use of their data, particularly 'sensitive' data.
- You should think about making provision to record the source of the information and any disclosure of it. This is not always relevant, but could be, especially if it is not obvious.
- You should think about how you date the creation and updating of records, to help you comply with the requirements that information be up-to-date and not held longer than necessary.
- By extension, you may need to think about procedures for automatically removing or flagging information you are no longer sure about, or no longer need.
- Any database linked to the Web in any way, or designed to exchange data with other organisations, needs to take account of the restrictions on transferring information outside western Europe.
- You may need a flag which records whether you have told people that you are processing information about them, and why. (If not, you may need to insert the relevant statement into your next communication with them.)
- You should think about how you brief users, either on-screen, in training materials, or whatever, about what the data is for, how it can legitimately be used, and who is allowed to do what with it.

The Data Protection Commissioner is believed, at the time of writing, to be preparing a guide explaining how designers can build systems that allow users to comply with the law on Data Protection, and to encourage the application of privacy-enhancing technologies.

Briefings for staff and volunteers

The following model briefing sheet might be useful (with local adaptations) in briefing those staff and volunteers who just need the minimum introduction to the Data Protection Act.

When you HOLD personal data

- You are allowed to use it only for the purpose(s) for which it was originally obtained.
- You have to take good care of it. (Security must be 'appropriate'.)
- You have to use it 'fairly'.
- You must ensure that it is: adequate, relevant, not excessive, accurate, up to date if necessary, and not held longer than necessary.
- You are committing an offence if you get access to personal data you are not authorised to, or if you disclose it to people you are not supposed to 'knowingly or recklessly'.
- You are committing an offence if you sell personal data you are not entitled to.

When you OBTAIN personal data

- You must not deceive or mislead anyone.
- You have to make sure that the person you are getting the data from knows what organisation is collecting the data, and why and how the data will be used.
- If you get the data from someone other than the individual themselves (the 'Data Subject'), you have to make sure that the Data Subject knows as soon as practicable who is using their data and why and how it will be used.
- You may have to get consent from the Data Subject to use their data, particularly if it is in any of the 'sensitive' categories. ('Sensitive data' covers the Data Subject's racial or ethnic origin, religious or political beliefs, Trade Union membership, health, sex life or criminal record.)
- You may also have to offer them the chance to opt out of some uses of the data, such as direct marketing, disclosure to other organisations, or use for secondary purposes.

When you DISCLOSE personal data

- You have to check that the disclosure fits the purpose or purposes for which the data is being held.
- You have to check that the person you are disclosing the information to is authorised to have it.
- You have to check that the Data Subject is aware that this type of disclosure is possible, or that there is an overriding reason (such as a legal obligation).
- If you put personal data onto the Web, you nearly always need consent from the Data Subject.
- If you transfer data outside western Europe, special rules apply.

Data Subjects have new RIGHTS

- If you need a person's consent, you cannot use the data if they don't give consent (but you can explain the consequences of not giving it).
- You cannot use data for direct marketing of any goods or services if the Data Subject has told you not to.
- If you are phoning people at home for direct marketing you have to check that the number you are calling is not on a barred register.
- Data Subjects can ask to see all the personal data you hold on them, including manual files. Your organisation has 40 days to comply with the request.

17
Transitional protection

There is provision in the Act for a three-year transition period. However, this starts from when the Act was originally supposed to come into effect, 24 October 1998, and therefore expires on 23 October 2001.

During the transition period, *existing activities* (see below) may, in effect, continue to operate under terms similar to those of the 1984 Act. Some of the new Data Protection Principles don't apply (including the conditions for fair processing and sensitive data); the right to prevent direct marketing doesn't apply; and many activities are exempt altogether, including, of course, all manual systems.

The transitional protection applies to *systems*: you can continue to add new records or new information to an existing system, but if you make substantial changes to what you are doing, or start a new project or activity with its own information systems, the transitional provisions will not apply.

The complication is that 'existing' means 'existing on 23 October 1998'. Any activity started since then, even if it was started before the Act came into force on 1 March 2000, has to comply with the new Act immediately.

You can opt into the new system before you have to. The Data Protection Commissioner recommends that, in particular, it may be easier to transfer all your activities onto the new basis rather than running a 'dual' system where some of your activities come under the new regime while others are using the transitional arrangements.

There is a further transitional period of six years – to 23 October 2007 – before manual files which were *held* before 24 October 1998 have to comply with the Data Protection Principles regarding quality of data (the third, fourth and fifth Principles) and various other provisions of the new Act. This provides time to sort out your archives, but it is important to ensure that *any* information added to a manual system, even a pre-existing one, after 23 October 1998 is ready to comply with the new Act by 24 October 2001.

Because most activities have to comply with the new Act fully from 24 October 2001, it is well worth starting the process of bringing all activities into compliance straight away. For this reason the transitional provisions are not described here in detail.

Further information

It is the Data Protection Commissioner's intention to produce written guidance on various aspects of the Act, in response both to demand from enquirers and to her own priorities. The most useful source of further information is therefore the Commissioner.

Data Protection Commissioner
Wycliffe House
Water Lane
Wilmslow
Cheshire
SK9 5AF
Switchboard: 01625 545700   Fax: 01625 545510

Information: 01625 545745
Web: www.dataprotection.gov.uk
e-mail: mail@dataprotection.gov.uk

Notification: 01625 545740
Web: www.dpr.gov.uk
e-mail: mail@notification.demon.co.uk

Telephone Preference Service
5th floor
Haymarket House
1 Oxendon Street
London SW1Y 4EE
Tel: 020 7766 4420   Fax: 020 7976 1886
e-mail: tps@dma.org.uk
An information pack for tele-marketers who want to know more is available.
To register a phone line not to receive unsolicited marketing: 0845 070 0707
To register a business fax line not to receive unsolicited marketing: 0845 070 0702
To consult the register of phone or fax numbers that have barred tele-marketing: www.numbercheck.co.uk

Bates Wells & Braithwaite, the solicitors whose partner Stephen Lloyd has helped with this book, are at:
Cheapside House
138 Cheapside
London EC2V 6BB
Tel: 020 7551 7777

Many organisations operating within specific sectors have done work on the application of the Data Protection Act to their constituency. The following (in alphabetical order) are among those known to the author at the time of writing.

Direct Marketing Association
Haymarket House
1 Oxendon Street
London SW1Y 4EE
Tel: 020 7321 2525   Fax: 020 7321 0191
e-mail: dma@dma.org.uk

Comprehensive guidance on how the Act affects direct marketing is being prepared, in consultation with the Home Office and Data Protection Commissioner. When published, it will be available to non-members, but could be costly.

Federation of Independent Advice Centres
4 Dean's Court
St Paul's Churchyard
London EC4V 5AA
Tel: 020 7489 1800   Fax: 020 7489 1804
e-mail: national@fiac.org.uk
A briefing on the application of the Data Protection Act in advice agencies is in production.

Institute of Charity Fundraising Managers
208 Market Towers
Nine Elms Lane
London SW8 5NQ
Tel: 020 7627 3436
Web: www.icfm.org.uk
The ICFM has published guidance notes on the 1998 Data Protection Act, £2.50 to non-members.

London Advice Services Alliance
2nd floor, Universal House
88–94 Wentworth Street
London E1 7SA
Tel: 020 7377 2748
e-mail: info@lasa.org.uk
Web: www.lasa.org.uk
LAAS has published a series of guides which includes The 1998 Data Protection Act, *8 pages, April 2000, £5.00.*

Telephone Helplines Association
4 Dean's Court
St Paul's Churchyard
London EC4V 5AA
Tel: 020 7248 3388   Fax: 020 7248 3399
e-mail: info@helplines.org.uk
The THA is actively exploring the implications of the Act for those running confidential helplines.

Voluntary Arts Network
PO Box 200
Cardiff
CF5 1YH
Tel: 02920 395395   Fax: 02920 397397
e-mail: info@voluntaryarts.org
Web: www.voluntaryarts.org
The VAN has published Briefing No. 46: Data Protection Act 1998, *8 pages, April 2000.*

Training

Training courses are held by:

Directory of Social Change
24 Stephenson Way
London
NW1 2DP
Tel: 020 7209 4949   Fax: 020 7209 4130

A training guide is produced four times a year.

In addition, many local Councils for Voluntary Service organise training on how to comply with the Data Protection Act, and/or can give advice. If you do not already know your local CVS, contact:

National Association of Councils for Voluntary Service
3rd floor Arundel Court
177 Arundel Street
Sheffield
S1 2NU
Tel: 0114 278 6636   Fax: 0114 278 7004

Appendix A Limited companies and charities

There is frequently confusion among those who work in voluntary organisations which are also charities about the relationship between company registration and charity status. The following notes may be helpful.

Any organisation is either 'incorporated' or 'unincorporated'. There are several forms of incorporation, the commonest of which is to be a limited liability company.

A commercial company is likely to be 'limited by shares': the members of the company are shareholders. Each owns a part of the company and receives dividends if it makes a profit. Trading companies linked to voluntary organisations are likely to be limited by shares. Normally the shares (or single share) are all held by the parent voluntary organisation or by Trustees on its behalf.

For voluntary organisations themselves it is usually not appropriate to be limited by shares. They will most likely be 'limited by guarantee'. The members in this case do not own the company, but they sign up to guarantee a small fixed amount (often £1) if the organisation cannot pay its debts when it is wound up.

Limited liability, whether by share or by guarantee, means that if the company gets into debt, the individual members are unlikely to be held personally liable for the debt. In the vast majority of cases, all they will lose is the value of their shares or the amount of their guarantee.

All companies – whether limited by shares or by guarantee – are incorporated (which literally means 'made into a body'). Incorporation means that the company has its own legal existence. It can sign contracts, borrow money and be sued, as though it was a real person. For Data Protection purposes this means that a company can have all the duties and responsibilities of a Data Controller in its own right.

An 'unincorporated' organisation doesn't exist as a legal person. This means that technically it cannot properly meet the definition of a Data Controller. The Data Protection Commissioner has indicated that for day-to-day purposes she will normally accept Notification from an unincorporated association in its own name, and deal with it in other respects as a Data Controller. However, if it should ever come to legal action, this would most likely have to be taken against the Trustees individually.

Charity status is a completely separate issue. A charity may be incorporated as a company limited by guarantee, or it may be unincorporated. The issue in either case is whether its purposes are wholly charitable. If they are, it is a charity, with all the consequent obligations under charity law, including the requirement to register with the Charity Commission in most cases. If the purposes are not wholly charitable, it cannot be a charity, even should it wish to be.

If you are in any doubt about your organisation's status, you need to refer to the governing document. For a limited company this will be its 'Memorandum and Articles of Association'. For an unincorporated association it will probably be a 'Constitution' or 'Rules'. For a trust (a form of unincorporated organisation) it will be a 'Trust Deed' or 'Declaration of Trust'.

The easiest way to find out if your organisation is a registered charity is to look on its headed paper. If it has a charity number or says 'Registered with the Charity Commission', the organisation is a registered charity. You can also look at the Register of Charities on the Charity Commission Web site (www.charity-commission.gov.uk.) and see if your organisation is listed. If you are still in doubt about whether the organisation is charitable – or if you think it should be registered with the Charity Commission but is not – contact the Charity Commission for further advice. Note that some charities are registered with the Inland Revenue rather than the Charity Commission. The Charity Commission can advise about this.

Charitable status has no effect at all on your Data Protection responsibilities, although various special provisions for *non-profit* organisations are described in the text of this book.

The Charity Commission works from three offices, in London, Liverpool and Taunton. If you already know which office covers your charity, use that contact. If not, use the national phone number, 0870 333 0123, or the Web site (see above).

Appendix B 'Schedule 3' *Conditions for processing sensitive personal data*

1. The data subject has given his explicit consent to the processing of the personal data.

2. (1) The processing is necessary for the purposes of exercising or performing any right or obligation which is conferred or imposed by law on the data controller in connection with employment.

   (2) The Secretary of State may by order –
      (a) exclude the application of sub-paragraph (1) in such cases as may be specified, or
      (b) provide that, in such cases as may be specified, the condition in sub-paragraph (1) is not to be regarded as satisfied unless such further conditions as may be specified in the order are also satisfied.

3. The processing is necessary –
   (a) in order to protect the vital interests of the data subject or another person, in a case where –
      (i) consent cannot be given by or on behalf of the data subject, or
      (ii) the data controller cannot reasonably be expected to obtain the consent of the data subject, or
   (b) in order to protect the vital interests of another person, in a case where consent by or on behalf of the data subject has been unreasonably withheld.

4. The processing –
   (a) is carried out in the course of its legitimate activities by any body or association which –
      (i) is not established or conducted for profit, and
      (ii) exists for political, philosophical, religious or trade-union purposes,
   (b) is carried out with appropriate safeguards for the rights and freedoms of data subjects,
   (c) relates only to individuals who either are members of the body or association or have regular contact with it in connection with its purposes, and
   (d) does not involve disclosure of the personal data to a third party without the consent of the data subject.

5. The information contained in the personal data has been made public as a result of steps deliberately taken by the data subject.

6. The processing –
   (a) is necessary for the purpose of, or in connection with, any legal proceedings (including prospective legal proceedings),

(b) is necessary for the purpose of obtaining legal advice, or

(c) is otherwise necessary for the purposes of establishing, exercising or defending legal rights.

7. (1) The processing is necessary –

    (a) for the administration of justice,

    (b) for the exercise of any functions conferred on any person by or under an enactment, or

    (c) for the exercise of any functions of the Crown, a Minister of the Crown or a government department.

(2) The Secretary of State may by order –

    (a) exclude the application of sub-paragraph (1) in such cases as may be specified, or

    (b) provide that, in such cases as may be specified, the condition in sub-paragraph (1) is not to be regarded as satisfied unless such further conditions as may be specified in the order are also satisfied.

8. (1) The processing is necessary for medical purposes and is undertaken by –

    (a) a health professional, or

    (b) a person who in the circumstances owes a duty of confidentiality which is equivalent to that which would arise if that person were a health professional.

(2) In this paragraph 'medical purposes' includes the purposes of preventative medicine, medical diagnosis, medical research, the provision of care and treatment and the management of healthcare services.

9. (1) The processing –

    (a) is of sensitive personal data consisting of information as to racial or ethnic origin,

    (b) is necessary for the purpose of identifying or keeping under review the existence or absence of equality of opportunity or treatment between persons of different racial or ethnic origins, with a view to enabling such equality to be promoted or maintained, and

    (c) is carried out with appropriate safeguards for the rights and freedoms of data subjects.

(2) The Secretary of State may by order specify circumstances in which processing falling within sub-paragraph (1)(a) and (b) is, or is not, to be taken for the purposes of sub-paragraph (1)(c) to be carried out with appropriate safeguards for the rights and freedoms of data subjects.

10. The personal data are processed in circumstances specified in an order made by the Secretary of State for the purposes of this paragraph.

Selected additional conditions laid down by regulation

Under Condition 10 above, The Secretary of State has issued Statutory Instrument 2000 No. 417, the Data Protection (Processing of Sensitive Personal Data) Order 2000. This contains a range of provisions, including the following which may be particularly relevant to voluntary organisations.

Circumstances in which sensitive personal data may be processed

4. The processing –
   (a) is in the substantial public interest;
   (b) is necessary for the discharge of any function which is designed for the provision of confidential counselling, advice, support or any other service; and
   (c) is carried out without the explicit consent of the data subject because the processing –
      (i) is necessary in a case where consent cannot be given by the data subject,
      (ii) is necessary in a case where the data controller cannot reasonably be expected to obtain the explicit consent of the data subject, or
      (iii) must necessarily be carried out without the explicit consent of the data subject being sought so as not to prejudice the provision of that counselling, advice, support or other service.

7. (1) Subject to the provisions of sub-paragraph (2), the processing –
      (a) is of sensitive personal data consisting of information falling within section 2(c) or (e) of the Act;
      (b) is necessary for the purpose of identifying or keeping under review the existence or absence of equality of opportunity or treatment between persons
         (i) holding different beliefs as described in section 2(c) of the Act, or
         (ii) of different states of physical or mental health or different physical or mental conditions as described in section 2(e) of the Act, with a view to enabling such equality to be promoted or maintained;
      (c) does not support measures or decisions with respect to any particular data subject otherwise than with the explicit consent of that data subject; and
      (d) does not cause, nor is likely to cause, substantial damage or substantial distress to the data subject or any other person.
   (2) Where any individual has given notice in writing to any data controller who is processing personal data under the provisions of

sub-paragraph (1) requiring that data controller to cease processing personal data in respect of which that individual is the data subject at the end of such period as is reasonable in the circumstances, that data controller must have ceased processing those personal data at the end of that period.

9. The processing –
   (a) is in the substantial public interest;
   (b) is necessary for research purposes (which expression shall have the same meaning as in section 33 of the Act);
   (c) does not support measures or decisions with respect to any particular data subject otherwise than with the explicit consent of that data subject; and
   (d) does not cause, nor is likely to cause, substantial damage or substantial distress to the data subject or any other person.

Appendix C The 1997 Police Act and criminal records

Under the 1984 Data Protection Act some employers have been checking job candidates' criminal records by requiring them to apply for Subject Access to their own records and provide a copy to the prospective employer. This has not been illegal, although it is not regarded as good practice, since the Subject Access request can reveal information such as 'spent' convictions, which the Data Subject would normally be able to keep secret.

The 1998 Data Protection Act makes it illegal to force anyone to make a Subject Access request. However, this provision comes into effect only when an alternative means of checking someone's criminal record becomes operational under the 1997 Police Act. This is now not expected in England and Wales before 2001 for the most sensitive occupations, and not before 2002 for the remainder. In Scotland the certificates should be available sooner.

The Police Act provides for three levels of certificate.

- A **Criminal Conviction Certificate** can be obtained by the individual, and will show only 'unspent' convictions. It is expected to cost around £10, which the prospective employer may choose to refund (as some currently do with Subject Access requests).
- A **Criminal Record Certificate** will show cautions and 'spent' convictions as well as 'unspent' convictions. It will apply to occupations which are exceptions under the 1974 Rehabilitation of Offenders Act such as teaching, medicine and security. This kind of certificate will be issued jointly to employers and individuals, but the employer must be registered with the new Criminal Records Bureau and must follow a Code of Practice.
- An **Enhanced Criminal Record Certificate** will include additional material, including acquittals and police intelligence, and will be available for a small number of jobs such as regular unsupervised work with children.